SPRINGS OF LOVE

by

Anna B. Mow

The Brethren Press, Elgin, Illinois

Cover design by Wendell Mathews
Cover photo by David Muench

Scriptural quotations unless otherwise noted are from the Revised Standard
Version of the Bible, copyrighted 1946, 1952, 1971, 1973 by the Division of
Christian Education of the National Council of the Churches of Christ in the
U.S.A. and used by permission.

Library of Congress Cataloging in Publication Data
Mow, Anna B
  Springs of love.

  Bibliography: p.
  1. Meditations. I. Title.
BV4832.2.M68   242   79-11186
ISBN 0-87178-810-1

Published by The Brethren Press, Elgin, Illinois 60120

Distributed by The Two Continents Publishing Group, LTD.
171 Madison Avenue, New York, New York 10016

Contents

PART THREE—The Gifts of the Spirit

PART FOUR—The Fruit of the Spirit and New Life

PART FIVE—*Questions That Bother People*

PREFACE

This book is dedicated to the late Mike Hoal. For several years he was disillusioned about the institutional church. Then I met him again. I promised to write a book for his need. He doesn't need my book now, for after a freak accident, facing death, he found the Lord and the true church. With joy he went to be with his Lord, asking family and friends to celebrate, not to mourn.

I am grateful to Eugenia Price for invaluable help in all my writing.

Anna B. Mow
Roanoka, Virginia

FOREWORD

I have had little confusion, few recurring doubts, no uneasiness over the mystery of the Holy Spirit's work and Presence in human life and there is a specific reason why I have not: for most of the years in which I have followed Jesus Christ, I have known and listened to Anna Mow. In all honesty, I can tell you that I have read no books, heard no sermons, no teaching which more clearly delineate in down to earth, understandable language the enormous potential of the indwelt life. I am overjoyed that Anna has at last set down these truths.

This singular woman of God *is*—Anna to me. One of God's great gifts has been her close and abiding friendship for well over a quarter of a century. She is a peacemaker—among Christians, in particular. Many of us would like to be just that, but Anna's facile mind, her ageless insights—her own Spirit-guided daily life give her a Divine "hand up" in this often prickly work. Dogmatic, varying viewpoints on the time of coming, the duration of the stay, the actual work of the Holy Spirit have divided Christians to a degree that causes me to sit and wonder. Because of what I have learned from Anna, I am certain that there is no need for such divisiveness, because God Himself is not divided and His Spirit—if understood at all clearly—will keep us posted as to God's nature and His eternal commitment to us all.

But, no one can deny that there *is* divisiveness. I predict this book will end at least some of it.

If I try for anything in my own thinking concerning Christian authenticity, it is to avoid dramatizing the direct action of the Spirit of God upon any human life. I do not dismiss out of hand a vision or a highly emotional experience, but Anna has taught me—by her words both spoken and written—and mainly by her life, to "test the spirits" which may bring about these experiences. She has year by year intensified my own longing for *sanity* and *balance*. She has been able to do this, not only because *she* is so sane and natural and balanced, but because long ago, she convinced me of the holy truth of what she has written in these pages.

Our mutual friend, the late E. Stanley Jones said often: "Jesus Christ was all sanctity, but He was also all *sanity*." I'm sure that his long years of association with Anna Mow helped convince Brother Stanley further.

In this book, you can find the road to *spiritual sanity*.

Anna has seen into the depths of the nature of the Holy Spirit. She is on target.

Of course, her amazing intellect helps, but with all my heart, I believe that Anna's Divine common sense concerning the Holy Spirit and us, springs from the authenticity of her own life lived with Him.

If you have read what I have written here, you hold in your hands a key to unlock much of the mystery, the possible perplexity or anxiety or confusion which you may have about your own relationship with God through His Holy Spirit.

With every Anna Mow book I read, I long for all her readers to be able to *hear* (as I can hear) the love and the caring and the delight in God which permeates her speaking voice—and especially her laughter. Read her slowly and carefully. *Listen* carefully. To "hear" my beloved friend, Anna, is an experience in itself. More important, if you "listen" well to what she has written, you will hear the voice of God.

Eugenia Price
St. Simons Island, Georgia

INTRODUCTION

Arnold Toynby, the great British historian, said some years ago that in a thousand years historians discussing our era will not list as the greatest issues those of capitalism and communism, or racial strife, but what happened when for the first time Christianity and Buddhism began to penetrate one another deeply.

A young minister asked me, "What do you think of Zen Buddhism?" I said, "I have been interested in Zen Buddhism and other mysticisms of the East for years, but have you heard about the Holy Spirit?" Americans who have never taken God's promises seriously and have been undisciplined in their lives, of course, find great benefit from seriously practicing quiet times and from accepting disciplines for their lives. A guru from India is reported to be persuading 30,000 converts a month to his method of finding inner peace. He promises relaxation with alertness, decreased blood pressure, decreased anxiety, increased individual self-esteem and capacity for intimate contact, increased creativity and personal satisfaction in life and work.

On the other hand, I know many Hindus who were previously devout in the faith they inherited but later found it inadequate. When these people found the reality of Christianity they gladly accepted the new truth even when it meant disinheritance and persecution. We need not be frightened about the inroads of foreign faiths if we know what we really have in Christ. I like Thomas Merton's attitude. Amiya Chakravarty wrote in *The Asian Journal of Thomas Merton* (page VII): Readers of Thomas Merton know that "his openness to man's spiritual horizons came from a *rootedness of faith* and *inner security* which led him to explore, experience, and interpret the affinities and differences between religion in the light of his own religion." Most people turn to Eastern faiths out of their own insecurities because they have never taken Christianity seriously.

The meditations in this book aim to help all of us see the whole truth as revealed in Christ. There is an answer for all anxieties and suffering. There is fulfillment for all emptiness. Christian meditation is never an end in itself; it is a coming into the presence of the living Lord to receive undreamed blessing from Him. It is coming to the God *without* Who wants to be the God *within* through His Holy Spirit. It is high time we take our own faith seriously.

PART ONE

*God's Promise
In The Old Testament*

1

OUR FATHER GOD

A Buddhist judge, a refugee from Vietnam, was a guest in a young minister's home. One day while using his host's typewriter he suddenly said, "Christians have a Father; all other religions are orphans. We are very lonely." This man was doubly lonely because he had to escape his native land without his wife and children. When we were on furlough from India in 1931-32 and I was still puzzled about the uniqueness of Christianity, I went to Dr. Charles Gilkey of the University Chapel in Chicago for help. I asked my question in a better way than I realized at that time. I asked, "Just how personal is God?" Dr. Gilkey shared many experiences out of his life, including questions that had come to him. Then he grasped the arms of his chair and exclaimed, "But I can never let go of the personality of God." Somehow his determined faith gave me the insight I needed at that time. Since then I know that that is the crux of the difference—the personality of God.

Jesus called God "Father" and knew Him in a *personal relationship*. If he is our Father, we are His children! He is more than an idea. He is more than whatever is inside of me as a human being. He is personal. He is known only through love. It is only to one's intellect that He may be incomprehensible; to the heart He can be understood.

A loving Father listens. We can talk anything over with Him.
Try it.

OUR GOD IS LOVE

Beloved, let us love one another; for love is of God, and he who loves is born of God and knows God. He who does not love does not know God; for God is love.   (I John 4:7,8.)

Love is a relationship word. As Christians we have failed more in this God characteristic than in any other way. A witness in word only, no matter how "orthodox," is not a Christian witness unless given in love. Even Mahatma Gandhi saw this. He loved the New Testament. He said, "Jesus lived in vain if He did not teach us to regulate the whole of life by the eternal law of love."

Meditate on I Cor. 13:4-7. The Apostle Paul gave this love as the basic test of one's experience of God. Perhaps the hardest characteristic of all is: "Love does not insist on its own way." We love one another by putting the best welfare of another ahead of our own. There is a song called *Love Is A Verb*. The Greek word of this love is *agape*. This is really an action word and not a *feeling* word. In this way only do we truly witness for our loving God.

In your meditation substitute "I" for the word "love" in each phrase of I Cor. 13:4-7. Then pray for whatever you need.

LOVE BEGINS WITH GOD

In this is love, not that we loved God but that He loved us. (I John 4:10.)

We love, because He first loved us. (I John 4:19.)

A Brahmin friend of ours in India gave up everything—wealth, family, and friends—to go out into the forest to find God. For thirteen years he sought desperately without a sense of having found anything. Then one day he discovered a copy of the Sermon on the Mount; later, a whole New Testament, and then a friend who led him to Christ. Years after having been a pastor of the Christian church in the midst of a Hindu holy city where he had once been a priest, I came to know him. One day when he visited us he said to me, "For thirteen years I tried to find God and then I found that He was seeking me all the time and that all I had to do was to respond to Him."

Too many Christians think that their salvation and progress as Christians depends on their own efforts. I was in a church in which a Sunday School class was named "The Seekers." I said, "Haven't you found anything yet?" Before I left them they changed their name.

Yes, seek we must. "Seek and ye shall find." But that kind of seeking is not desperate human effort; it is really an openness to the loving God who waits for us to come to Him. I heard the late great Martin Buber of Israel say, "God comes in wherever He is let in." This is a basic Bible truth. God seeks us long before we seek Him.

Be quiet for ten minutes in His presence *and think about His waiting love. Tell Him all your doubts and longings—and* listen.

GOD TAKES THE INITIATIVE TOWARD US

The Word of God in the Bible dared to face religion as well as science in its environment, and borrow their patterns, not in order to copy them, but to use them for the communication of a radically novel message which by repercussion has transformed them radically, showing that *human efforts to "God" are replaced by God's coming to man*.
(Page 171 in *The Meaning of The Old Testament* by Lys.)

The wonder of it is that God wants us more than we can ever want Him. On first reading the Bible, people of other faiths see the wonder of this truth. It takes all the strain out of their seeking. Times of silence in meditation are even more important for a Christian. It is not only the healing quiet that is important, but the listening to a God of love, a great Other who is always reaching out to everyone with love. Unless we listen we cannot hear. The Bible people heard Him. We have the same God and we know more about Him than all the Old Testament people.

Be still and know that I am God. (Ps. 46:10.)

For God alone my soul waits in silence;
  for my hope is from Him.
He only is my rock and salvation,
  my fortress; I shall not be shaken.

(Ps. 62:5,6.)

Indeed "God comes in whenever He is let in."
Listen to His message for you.

THE MIRACLE OF FAITH

By faith Abraham obeyed when he was called to go out to a place which he was to receive as an inheritance; and he went out, not knowing where he was to go.   (Heb. 11:8.)

Next to the coming of Jesus perhaps the greatest religious miracle of all time was in how Abraham came to such a faith in the one God. He lived in an idolatrous country and his own father made idols. The intriguing question is, how did Abraham even come to the consciousness of a God with whom he could even have conversation and to whom he could trust his life? He banked everything in his life on this faith in one personal God. In fact, the whole Bible story is of people whose faith was proved real in this one God. They believed that He knew what was best for them, and whenever they were faithful to Him they found life to be good. They found that they could talk to Him and they could hear what He wanted them to do.

In fact, the Old Testament prayer references cannot be found in a concordance because more often it is not called "prayer" but it says "God said to Abraham" and "Abraham said to God."

With all the Bible evidence before us, we need not be afraid to have faith in this One God.

Christian meditation starts with thoughts of this God who is our heavenly Father, rather than with merely hunting for a god inside of us. Meditation is coming into His Presence—to listen.

Worship and adore Him in your own words
or in silence.

GOD CALLS BY NAME

And the angel of the Lord appeared to him in a flame of fire out of the midst of a bush; and he looked, and lo, the bush was burning, yet it was not consumed. And Moses said, "I will turn aside and see this great sight, why the bush was not burnt." When the Lord saw that he turned aside to see, God called to him out of the bush, "Moses, Moses!"

(Ex. 3:2-4.)

Although Moses was a Hebrew, he was reared by the princess of Egypt in the royal household and educated as a royal son. His mother was his nurse and must have done her best in teaching him about his own people. (Read Exodus Chapters 1 and 2.) As a young man, he turned to his people and in trying to help them in their slavery he got into trouble with the authorities and had to flee into the desert. He became a herdsman in the desert. The silence of the desert was a formidable contrast to the life in the royal household, but Moses must have learned some of his life's greatest lessons there. In that wild silence he heard his name called and he responded. Out of this experience came one of the greatest stories of a man and his relationship to a personal God. Even in our day it was counted spectacular enough to be made into a movie.

As Moses responded to God it was no longer a desert silence but an inner quiet in his heart which remained with him throughout his strenuous life. His whole life became a response to a very personal God.

Have you had quiet enough to listen for your name being called?
What do you think God wants to say to you?
Take ten minutes, at least, to listen and to say, "Here am I."

GOD OR GODS

In the early days of Israel there was a constant conflict between the idea of a personal God and the gods of nature which the people of Canaan worshiped. On Mount Carmel the prophet Elijah challenged the people to make a real choice to decide between the God of Moses and the Canaanite gods. (Read I Kings 18:20-39). For that day they chose God, but, as the years passed, the people of God's chosen nation lost the way many times.

The subtlest religious perversion was the hypocrisy of a ritualized worship which was glaringly inconsistent with a moral God. The people often forgot the sole sovereignty of God. They forgot the ethical nature of their personal God and the requirement to be moral in their own lives. In centering on the current type of religious experience of their neighbors they even forgot God's promise of hope for the future in a coming Messiah. Even to the time of Jesus this was often true. On His final trip to Jerusalem Jesus cried out:

O Jerusalem, Jerusalem, killing the prophets and stoning those who are sent to you! How often would I have gathered your children together as a hen gathers her brood under her wings, and you would not! (Matt. 23:37.)

There is little difference in any worship of any religion when it is centered only in self-conscious feeling and experience.

Do I ever forget God and my relationship with Him and center down instead on my feeling in "worship?"

In silence, concentrate on the God who loves you and wants relationship with you.

PART TWO

The Gift of the Spirit . . .
. . . As Jesus Taught It (9-24)
. . . As Promised (25-36)

GOD WITH US

He was born in an obscure village,
the child of a peasant woman.
He grew up in still another village,
where He worked in a carpenter shop
until He was thirty. Then for three
years He was an itinerant preacher.
He never wrote a book, He never held
an office. He never had a family or
owned a house. He didn't go to college.
He never visited a big city. He never
traveled two hundred miles from the place
where He was born. He did none of the
things one usually associates with greatness.
He had no credentials but Himself. He was
only thirty-three when the tide of public
opinion turned against Him. His friends ran
away. He was turned over to His enemies and
went through the mockery of a trial. He was
nailed to a cross between two thieves. While
He was dying, His executioners gambled for His
clothing, the only property He had on earth.
When He was dead, He was laid in a borrowed grave through
the pity of a friend. Nineteen centuries have come and
gone, and today He is the central figure of the human
race and the leader of human progress.

All the armies that have ever marched, all the navies
that ever sailed, all the parliaments that ever sat,
all the kings that ever reigned, put together, have not
affected the life of man on earth as that *One Solitary
Life*.

This man is our Loving Lord through whom we have our
relationship with God. Thinking about Him is *Transforming Meditation*.

O Lord, I come to be Yours only.
I trust You with all my life.
Amen.

13

TO BE TRUSTED WITH POWER

On the last day of the feast, the great day, Jesus stood up and proclaimed, "If any one thirst, let him come to me and drink. He who believes in me out of his heart shall flow rivers of living water."

Now this He said about the Spirit, which those who believed in Him *were* to receive; for as yet the Spirit had not been given, because Jesus was not yet glorified.   (John 7:37-39.)

Jesus said there was a coming of the Holy Spirit to be dated in history. From the beginning of history the Holy Spirit had been at work in the world. Now something new was going to happen. One at once wonders what this means. What will be different?

Just before His ascension, Jesus told His disciples that they would receive *power* when the Holy Spirit came upon them. (Acts 1:8.) The Greek word for power used here is the same word from which we get the words *dynamo* and *dynamite*. This is power indeed and one must know how to use such power.

A very active church woman said to me after Bible study on the Holy Spirit, "Why don't I have the Holy Spirit?" I said, "The Spirit is power. If you had the power what would you do with it?" She answered, "If I had the power——, if I had the power I would get rid of all the people who are blocking progress in the church." I said, "That is exactly why God hasn't given power to you. He wants to *win* all those people because He loves them."

This is why Jesus had to come first before such power could be given to mankind, so we would understand that God power is also love power.

Meditate on love as one side of God's power. How did Jesus show that?

A SPRING OR A CISTERN?

When Jesus was talking about inner springs in John 7:37-39 He was talking about infinite resources for any need in living. I imagine that the thought of inner springs brought to mind the Lord's message through Jeremiah (2:11-13).

Has a nation changed its gods,
  even though they are no gods?
But my people have changed their glory
  for that which does not profit.

Be appalled, O heavens, at this,
  be shocked, be utterly desolate, says the Lord.
For my people have committed two evils;
  they have forsaken me,
the fountain of living water,
  and hewed out cisterns for themselves,
broken cisterns,
  that can hold no water.

Cisterns have no inner source of water; they are dependent entirely on rainfall. In times of drought they are empty. When people depend only on their own human resources or think they can find God by their own efforts, they turn out to be empty cisterns. This can happen also to people who have already known the power of God through the Holy Spirit. It is always a temptation to turn back to self-centeredness. For the experienced Christian this is revealed by spiritual pride, arrogance, being hard on others, lack of love and, if criticized, a feeling of being persecuted. This is changing the glory of God for that which does not profit.

O Father, keep me in Thy love so I never stray from the center of Thy will. Amen.

JESUS' LAST WILL AND TESTAMENT

Jesus, knowing that the Father had given all things into His hands, and that he had come from God and was going to God, rose from supper, laid aside his garments, and girded Himself with a towel. (John 13:3.)

World power is always *over* other people, but God power is *for* other people. Jesus had to live among us to get this message across. He had lived among the people as a servant. "He did not count equality with God a thing to be grasped, but emptied himself, taking the form of a servant. . . ." (Phil. 2:6-8). So on this last night with His disciples before His death He washed their feet. They did not yet understand this law of the Kingdom of God. They still expected the Messiah to be their political deliverer from the occupying control of Rome. No wonder Peter protested. Their Lord and Master a servant! (When the law of servanthood is forgotten, any group, even if called "Christian," becomes a cult. This is what happened to the cult in Guyana which even led to a mass suicide/murder.)

But before Jesus gave them His last will and testament He had to do what He could to help them understand this law of servanthood. It seems that the basic human fear is that someone will walk over us. Such a fear takes away all inner security. Jesus came to show us that inner security comes through a new relationship to God. This inner security comes through the Holy Spirit of God which Jesus was getting His disciples ready to receive.

On this last night they had their Passover meal together and, after He washed their feet, He was ready to tell them about what was going to happen.

When we observe "holy communion" we are not only representing the death of Jesus but we are also accepting our part in His last will and testament for us.

Meditate on the meaning of servanthood which is not being a slave but is real freedom.

A NEW COMMANDMENT

A new commandment I give to you, that you love one another; even as I have loved you, that you also love one
another. By this will all men know that you are my disciples,
if you have love for one another.   (John 13:34)

This is not a legalistic command like the commands worked out
in the old law. It is a personal response to the prior love of God.

Beloved, let us love one another; for love is of God, and he
who loves is born of God and knows God. He who does not
love does not know God; for GOD IS LOVE. (I John 4:19.)

We love because He first loved us. (I John 4:19.) This love
casts out fear. (I John 4:18.) It is the heart of true servanthood,
because it is for the best welfare of the others. Self-centeredness
is the basic biblical sin. We live in God's love when we put God
and others above our own selves. This love discipline has been the
hardest lesson for Christians through the ages to learn, because
we have not learned the secret of servanthood.

Thirty years ago two young men from Afghanistan were brought
to an Indian dinner at our house in Chicago. I knew that
Christianity was not permitted in their country and that these
men were sent here by their government. They would never
come to a missionary's home in India but they were coming to us
in Chicago. I spent three days cooking everything a Moslem
would like, as my Christian opportunity with them. One of these
men became like a son to us. But after two years in America he
was at a meeting for foreign students at Brent House when he was
asked to share anything out of his experience. He said he came to
America absolutely opposed to Christianity but has now changed
his mind. But he was also convinced, after being in America two
years, that, if one Christian group came to his country, another
would come, and they would be in conflict with one another. We
have friends who were in Kabul when the first Christian Church
was built there. They saw the police tear the church down brick
by brick.

*How we fail our Lord when we do not have God love!
Examining our own reactions to others in the light of God's
love for us should help us to greater faithfulness.*

PRAYER POWER

Truly, truly, I say to you, he who believes in me will also do the works that I do; and greater works than these will he do, because I go to the Father. Whatever you ask in my name, I will do it, that the Father may be glorified in the Son; if you ask anything in my name, I will do it.   (John 14:12-14.)

It is astounding that Jesus made such a promise, even that we would do greater works than He had done! He knew that this would be possible only through the Holy Spirit power which would be given after He was gone to the Father. The requests must be in His name and must glorify the Father in the Son. Self-centered requests are not included in this promise.

The first time I really took this promise seriously was one spring in Landour, India. Our Bulsar "Christian" boys had a terrible reputation among the Hindus of our city, and many of them had earned it. I had the work among the women and the girls, but no man was free to work with the males. I was concerned, but I found that I had not even prayed for these boys for fear God would ask me to do something for them. Reading Jesus' promise challenged me and I began to pray. When I got back home I knew I had to do something. Finally, I decided I could at least have a tea party for the boys without criticism. I called one of the older youth and told him what I felt. I asked him if the boys would come. He said, "I don't know but I'll find out." The next day he told me they wanted to come. The time was set tor 8 p.m. ten days later.

The die was cast and I waited. All I knew was that I had to do something.

On the next page I'll finish the story. The point for meditation here is that *if* we believe, the time comes to *act*.

I believe; help Thou my unbelief!

SURPRISE ANSWERS

The word got out that I was having a party for the boys and many people came to warn me of trouble. "Will you serve with your good cups?" and all such questions were asked. "If they break the cups, I'll get more," I answered. For nine days people continued to warn me. The day before the party three of the fellows came and asked to have an hour of the evening. I told them to take the first hour. I thought if they spoiled it, I could do something about it.

The evening arrived and I was ready with games that could not get rowdy and with refreshments. And I hoped by the end of the evening we could sing some hymns and close with prayer. Then five minutes of eight and no one in sight! Were they coming?

At 8 o'clock on the minute, twenty-six young men arrived dressed in their best clothes and carrying Bibles and hymn books under their arms! Their leader asked for a stand and then called on me to pray. I had just come from the hills where we used our second language. I got three languages mixed up, but at least God knew my overjoyed heart! After their part of the program, which was very spiritual, my planned games did not suit. We had the refreshments and then we talked. They wanted to come again. We planned for a Bible study every Sunday night. Out of that Bible hour and fellowship came two churchwide revivals, born-again young men, evangelists and pastors—and much glory to God.

God may ask for small action but He adds the miracles.

THE PROMISE

I will pray the Father, and He will give you another Counselor, to be with you forever, even the Spirit of truth, whom the world cannot receive, because it neither sees him nor knows him; you know him, for he dwells with you AND WILL BE IN YOU.   (John 14:16,17.)

Even though the prophet Joel (2:18-32) said that God would pour out his Spirit upon all flesh, the disciples did not understand the meaning of this promise until the Day of Pentecost (Acts 2:17-21). They were still thinking of the human Jesus whom they had fully accepted as their Messiah. In their limited thinking Jesus must be ready to come into the fullness of His power and they could not yet conceive of death for Him. On this last night with them, He told them He would not leave them desolate but He would come to them. But they did not yet see that He was coming to them through the Holy Spirit. He said, "Yet a little while, and the world will see me no more, but you will see me; because I live, you will live also. In that day you will know that I am in my Father, and you in me and I in you" (John 14:19,20).

Three times Jesus had told His disciples about his coming death *and resurrection* but they did not understand. After the third announcement James and John came to Him and asked for special favor, to be placed one on His right and one on His left in the coming kingdom. They were asking for honor, as well as crowding out Peter, who was the third in their inner circle. Jesus told them they did not know what they were asking. Then Jesus talked to them about servanthood (Mark 10:32-45).

Days of tragedy and despair were coming but they did not know that yet, either.

All they knew at this stage was that Jesus was their Master and their promised Messiah.

We can ask ourselves: "Do we love Jesus enough to be carried through the times when we cannot understand what is happening?"

THE GIFT OF PEACE

Peace I leave with you, my peace I give to you. Let not your hearts be troubled, neither let them be afraid.

(John 14:27.)

The peace of Jesus which He offers as a gift is almost unbelieveable. He knows what the disciples do not know, that He is to be murdered the next day. He was facing the most cruel suffering and death and still He could talk about peace. That is peace, indeed.

When we accept this gift of peace which He is relating to the gift of the Spirit, we enter into a new depth of faith. Our commitment to Him holds no matter what happens. It is not what happens to us but how we relate to what happens. The Apostle Paul had accepted this peace from God:

This priceless treasure we hold, so to speak, in a common earthenware jar—to show that the splendid power of it belongs to God and not to us. We are handicapped on all sides but we are never frustrated; we are puzzled but never in despair. We are persecuted, but we never have to stand it alone: we may be knocked down but we are never knocked out: . . .
We wish you could see how all this is working out for your benefit, and how the more grace God gives, the more thanksgiving will redound to His glory. This is the reason why we never collapse. (II Cor. 4:7-15, Phillips.)

When you keep your faith in Him "the peace of God, which passes all understanding, will keep your hearts and your minds in Christ Jesus" (Phil. 4:7).

Dear Lord, I look to Thee only in any circumstance and gladly accept your gift of peace through your Spirit which is also my priceless gift. Amen.

THE SPIRIT IS OUR LIFE

Abide in me and I in you. As the branch cannot bear fruit by itself, unless it abides in the vine, neither can you, unless you abide in me. I am the vine, you are the branches.

(John 15:5.)

This parable is about the Holy Spirit, telling us that Jesus is our life through the Holy Spirit. I have a modern parable. When we came back to Virginia we had two big cotton poplar trees in our front yard. They grew so fast that the electric light company had to come every two years to top them to keep them out of the wires. Also, besides that, their big leaves dropped all spring and summer, as well as in the fall. My husband got tired of picking up leaves all season, so one time he asked the men if they'd like to cut them down instead of topping them. They were delighted not to have to come again. They were so grateful they even cut up the trunks into logs for our fireplace. My husband carried the logs out to the back yard. Those crazy logs didn't know they were dead. They put out leaves and branches all the remainder of that summer! But after six years the few logs left were too rotten to carry in.

Too many people in the church are living off of leftover life. They are not connected to life and they wonder why they feel so empty. Many people are spiritually anemic but do not know why or what to do. For spiritual health go to the Source of life. He is the life and we must recognize His Presence. As long as we obey His commandments we abide in His love (John 15:10). He has done His part. The only thing that can break this connection is a refusal on our part to obey. He will never break the connection. Only we can do that. Our feelings are not the determining factor, only our choosing.

Thank God for LIFE.

THE NEW POSSIBILITY FOR GOD RELATIONSHIP

It is to your advantage that I go away, for if I do not go away, the Counselor will not come to you; but if I go, I will send him to you.   (John 16:7.)

He will glorify me, for he will take what is mine and declare it to you. All that the Father has is mine; therefore I said he will take what is mine and declare it to you.   (John 16:14, 15.)

Jesus was saying that the Holy Spirit was not merely a substitute for His absence, but would be the agent of His continued presence. All that He had been to His disciples was little compared to what He would be through the Holy Spirit.

Through the Holy Spirit Jesus would be more than an influence by their side. He would be the inner life of His followers. Jesus also pictured the Holy Spirit as an inner spring (John 7:37; cf. Jer. 2:13). He would be as the life coming to the branches from the vine (John 15). We know that a branch that is merely tied on to the vine cannot live; it must be *connected*.

This is relationship indeed, to be really connected to life in Christ. Jesus has done His part. He waits now for us to accept His offer of new life and infinite resources.

In preparation for better meditation and understanding, take the time to read the whole book of Acts through in one sitting. That is good home work for Christian meditation.

Come in, Lord Jesus?

CONVICTION: THE WORK OF THE HOLY SPIRIT

When he comes he will convince the world of sin and of
righteousness and of judgment.   (John 16:8.)

I suppose we in the church have failed more than in anything
else in our meddling in the work of the Holy Spirit. Pointing out
others' sins and blaming them has been our way of life and our
defense to cover our own failures. At women's retreats wives
confess their husbands' sins and shortcomings. Since I am the age
I am, I have been in men's retreats. Do you know what? They
confess their wives' sins. Parents tell me what's wrong with their
teenagers, and teenagers tell me where their parents have failed
them.

In a certain community the "town drunk" was converted and
was active in the church for a year. Then he slipped into his old
ways and did not return to the church out of shame because he
heard the prevailing criticism: "We knew he wouldn't last." The
pastor was full of the love of God. He found the man and kept in
touch with him in a most forgiving and loving way. After six
months I had meetings in that church. On Saturday night the man
returned for the first time after his "fall." After the meeting I was
talking to him while the pastor kept his arm around the man.
While we were talking a woman of the church came up to the man
and, pointing a finger at him, said accusingly, "Well, where have
you been all this time?" Thank God for that loving pastor.

Most young people lost to the church are away from the church
because of such criticism. Such criticism breaks courage.

I have seen many marriages restored when either mate takes his
or her fingers out of the work of the Spirit. We must stand by in
loving patience and make it easier for others to confess their own
sins. That is what Jesus did for people.

O Lord, I need this gift of love to be more like Thee.

A GUIDE AND TEACHER

I have yet many things to say to you, but you cannot bear them now. When the Spirit of truth comes, he will guide you into all truth, for he will not speak on his own authority, but whatever he hears he will speak, and he will declare to you the things that are to come. (John 16:12-13.)

But the Counselor, the Holy Spirit, whom the Father will send in my name, he will teach you all things, and bring to your remembrance all that I have said to you.

(John 14:26.)

There were many things they would not have understood even if He had explained them. We have no record that He ever told them how to be baptized. He left no plans for organization. He never told them that His followers would have to separate from the Jewish community. He never told them that the day would come when Gentiles would become Christians without first becoming Jews. This was the most traumatic experience in the history of the church. He never made statements about the place of women in the church which was to evolve.

If Jesus had made such statements, we would be looking back to see how to be faithful to His new *laws*. But Jesus came to show us how to have *relationship* with the Heavenly Father, even like His relationship. Jesus wanted His disciples to know that, even when He was gone from them as they knew Him, He would still be with them through the promised Holy Spirit. And through the Spirit their relationship with Him would continue.

We are not left orphans; we have a Father and a Savior plus the Holy Spirit through whom this relationship is maintained.

Thank you, Heavenly Father, for such a relationship.

PRAYER FOR OUR UNITY

And now I am no more in the world, but they are in the world, and I am coming to thee. Holy Father, keep them in thy name which thou hast given me, that they may be one, even as we are one.   (John 17:11.)

Our unity is in Christ, in our *relationship* to Him and not only *in* Him. We do not make unity; we join it in Him. Our greatest witness is in loving fellowship with one another, even when we differ. The first time I spoke to the Mennonites at Harrisonburg, Virginia, I said I remembered the day when there was more rejoicing over a Mennonite becoming a Brethren than over a sinner becoming a Christian. After the meeting an old brother said to me, "You should have seen how we crowed when we got the Brethren!"

There are no clones in the family of God. There are no copycats. We are all different, and that variety makes life much more exciting.

Only our relationship to Christ can keep us in unity; otherwise we overemphasize our differences. Then arrogance breaks fellowship. It was arrogance of conscientious followers of the Law that led to the crucifixion of Jesus.

Our problem is to have deep conviction of truth and at the same time have the love of God in our hearts.

O Lord, keep us close to Thee so we can love one another.

SENT OUT BY JESUS

I do not pray that thou shouldst take them out of the world, but that thou shouldst keep them from the evil one. They are not of the world even as I am not of the world. Sanctify them in the truth; thy word is truth. As thou didst send me into the world, so I have sent them into the world.   (John 17:16-18.)

The human tendency is to seek those who agree with us and stay away from those who differ from us. When new groups huddle because of like ideas or like experiences they tend to become a cult. This is what makes a possible good idea into a perversion of fellowship. We need our own fellowships for growth, encouragement, and understanding, but we meet in order to have greater strength for going out. On the other hand, some people are peddlers of their own ideas without being sent by the Lord.

We are sent to represent our Lord in all His love and understanding. The experience in the Antioch church is a good example:

While they were worshiping the Lord and fasting, the Holy Spirit said, "Set apart for me Barnabas and Saul for the work to which I have called them." Then after fasting and praying they laid their hands on them and sent them off. So, *being sent out by the Holy Spirit, they went* . . . (Acts 13:2,3.)

God does not call us for our blessing only; He calls us to help all the other people to know Him. The biggest mistake by the people in the Old Testament was that they got the idea they were God's pets when they were all called to be God's priests. Even Abraham was called to be a blessing to all peoples.

The person sent out by the Lord is never alone, because the Lord is with him.

O Lord, help me always to hear Thy call.

DARKNESS

And when they had sung a hymn, they went out to the Mount of Olives. Then Jesus said to them, "You will all fall away because of me this night. . . ." (Matt. 26:30,31.)

It was night, a dark one, indeed! Judas must have thought that Jesus just didn't understand the way of the world. He would force his hand. He betrayed his Lord, but Jesus did not escape as he expected. His suicide was the measure of his plan's defeat. As the trials proceeded, nine of the disciples scattered, as Jesus knew they would; John was nearby watching what happened to Jesus. Peter was in the courtyard. He couldn't believe what was happening. In his despair and utter confusion he even denied his Lord. Not long before this he said he would die for his Lord! Now he was in a trance. He even denied his Lord three times, as Jesus had said. "And immediately, while he was still speaking, the cock crowed. And the Lord turned and *looked at Peter*. That look must have been one of love and compassion. Peter went out and wept bitterly (Luke 22:54-62).

Then they took Jesus and crucified Him, the most shameful and cruel death known in the Roman Empire.

For the disciples, so far as they could see, this was the end of all their hopes and dreams. They had been so sure He was their expected Messiah, and now He was dead!

Whenever Jesus had mentioned the cross it always bore His meaning, not theirs. He knew that the cross was not the end. It was only a new beginning.

We know that now. The Apostle Paul stated it for us:

For I delivered to you as of first importance what I also received, that Christ died for our sins in accordance with the scriptures, that he was buried, that he was raised on the third day in accordance with the scriptures . . . (I Cor. 15:3,4.)

HE DID ALL THAT FOR US. Thank you, Lord.

MORNING CAME! AND WONDERFUL LIGHT!

The women were first at the tomb on Sunday morning. They came to anoint His body. An "angel" met them and said:

Do not be amazed; you seek Jesus of Nazareth, who was crucified. He has risen; he is not here; see the place where they laid him. But go, tell his disciples *and Peter* that he is going before you to Galilee; there you will see him, as he told you.   (Luke 16:7.)

This news was as unbelievable as His death. But this was also true, gloriously true. Mary Magdalene ran to tell Peter and John. It was she who saw the risen Lord first. She cried, "I have seen the Lord!"

That same evening the disciples were gathered behind closed doors for fear of the Jews. "Jesus came and stood among them and said to them, 'Peace be with you.'" When he had said this he showed them his hands and his side. Then the disciples were glad when they saw the Lord. Jesus said to them again, "Peace be with you. As the Father has sent me, even so I send you." And when he had said this, he breathed on them, and said to them, "Receive the Holy Spirit. . . ." They still did not comprehend what all this meant.

As a child, I often tried to think how Jesus in His risen body could get through the walls. But I got the right idea when I saw this scene in the Passion Play in Zion, Illinois. All the time the one playing the part of Jesus was behind the half pillar in the back of the room. Then I realized that that is what happened on this Sunday evening with the disciples. *He was there all the time,* when they saw Him He had only made Himself visible to the human eyes.

After the resurrection, for forty days, they never knew when they would see Him. Paul lists many such appearances in writing to the Corinthians (I Cor. 15:4-8). They would see Him, then they wouldn't, until they got the feeling of His presence all the time.

Paul belongs to our era and even he had such an appearance. This has happened to many Christians through the years when they needed it.

Thank you for a risen Lord. Even when we don't see with our physical eyes we know by faith.

TARRYING FOR THE PROMISE

"And behold, I send the promise of my Father upon you; but stay in the city until you are clothed with power from on high." Then he led them out as far as Bethany, and lifting up his hands he blessed them. While he blessed them, he parted from them. And they *returned to Jerusalem full of joy*.

(Luke 24:49-52.)

To them he presented himself alive after his passion by many proofs, appearing to them during forty days, and speaking of the kingdom of God. And while praying with them he charged them not to depart from Jerusalem, but to *wait for the promise* of the Father, which, he said, "You heard from me, for John baptized with water, but before many days you shall be baptized with the Holy Spirit." (Jesus disappeared from their sight.) Then they returned to Jerusalem from the Mount called Olivet . . . they went to the upper room. . . . All these with one accord devoted themselves to prayer. . . .

(Acts 1:3-14.)

When Jesus disappeared from their sight in death, they were in utter despair. Now He disappeared from their physical sight again, but this time they were full of joy. Jesus had conquered death. He had explained the scriptures to them about Himself. They had seen and fellowshipped with Him in His risen body. It no longer mattered when they could not see Him. They knew He was alive.

Jesus had said something new was going to happen to them. They had never heard anyone tell an experience of Spirit baptism. But Jesus said something was going to happen. Their whole attention was on Him, not on themselves. One can imagine what those 120 people talked about while they waited.

On the day of Pentecost, the festival of first fruits, *it happened*. (Read Acts 2.) They were all filled with the Holy Spirit. A sound came like the rush of a mighty wind. Tongues of fire rested in each person's head. As the Spirit gave them utterance they spoke with other tongues. There were Jews in Jerusalem from many countries. They asked, "And how is it that we hear, each of us in his own language?" Peter answered the people as he preached his first sermon. When the people asked what they could do Peter answered, "Repent and be baptized everyone of you in the name of Jesus Christ for the forgiveness of your sins; and you shall receive the gift of the Holy Spirit for the promise is to you and to your children and to all that are afar off, everyone whom the Lord our God calls to him."

Thank you, Lord, that we are not left out.

THE REAL HAPPENING ON THE DAY OF PENTECOST

"They were all filled with the Holy Spirit," all 120 of them who had been in prayer for ten days (Acts 2). To know what really happened one must read the whole book of Acts. The manifestations of that day were nothing compared to what happened afterwards. On that very day 3,000 people were converted to Christianity. They all had a new love for one another. Wherever they found need they met it, even to fantastic healings. Non-Christians were amazed, but they praised God rather than the new Christians when these wonderful things happened, because they knew such results could never be expected from ordinary people. The Christians did not talk about their own feelings but about the wonder of the risen Lord.

I agree with Dr. Ernest White, a Christian psychiatrist in London, who said that the Holy Spirit on that day became an inner power rather than an outside influence. On that day He took up His abode in the unconscious. This was now the inner spring and the new life which Jesus had predicted. Paul had the same idea:

> For this reason I bow my knees before the Father, from whom every family in heaven and earth is named, that according to the riches of his glory he may grant you to be strengthened with might through *his Spirit in the inner man*, and that *Christ may dwell in your hearts by faith*; that you, being rooted and grounded in love, may have power to comprehend with all the saints what is the breadth and length and height and depth, and to know the love of Christ which surpasses knowledge, and that you may be *filled with all the fulness* of God. (Eph. 3:14-19.)

The *Spirit in one's inner being, Christ in me, filled with all the fulness of God*—all describe the same experience.

Peter said it is for all of us. (Acts 2:39.)

Thank God.

THE WONDER OF IT!

You are in the Spirit, if the Spirit of God really dwells in
you.   (Rom. 8:9.)

If the Holy Spirit's abode is in the innermost part of our person-
alities, then His work is basically quiet. The times I am guided
and do not know it are a greater challenge to me than when I know
the guidance in advance and follow it consciously. This is why our
relationship commitment must never be broken.

One such experience I shall never forget. In a large Michigan
retreat a box for questions was placed on the platform and opened
on Saturday evening. One question was, "How can I, a young
mother with three active children, find time to pray?" The
question was given to me. I do not remember the incident at all,
but two years later the young mother told me about it. According
to her report, I said I learned how to find time when I remembered
that prayer is first of all a relationship matter. Then she added,
"You said, 'So pray while you vacuum.'" I never liked that awk-
ward word "vacuum" and always avoided it. Here I used it
unselfconsciously. What I did not know, but the Holy Spirit did,
was that she had a new rug which she vacuumed three times a
day. She was also impatient with her children about the rug. At
the word "vacuum" she saw her problem and that minute dedicated her life to God anew. She said "from that time to this I am a
new woman." Who would ever dream that "vacuum" could be an
evangelistic word!

So close is this relationship with the Lord through the Holy
Spirit that we can be used in His service even when we do not
know it.

Thank Him for that.

FIRST PENTECOST RESULTS

When the people heard Peter's first sermon on the Day of Pentecost *they were cut to the heart*. The message was preached but the conviction came from the Holy Spirit. To the 120 who had already received the Holy Spirit on that day about 3000 more were added to the group! Imagine any church with 120 membership having 3000 new converts in one day! This looks like an impossible situation, but it was the work of the Spirit. Therefore, they all had so much love for one another that they sold all their possessions and goods and distributed to each as was needed. "And all who believed were together and had all things in common" (Acts 2:37-47). Day by day they attended the temple together and broke bread in their homes with glad and generous hearts. Many others continued to join this new fellowship.

No one was told he had to sell everything. It was done spontaneously out of the new love for one another. However, one couple, Ananias and Sapphira, after selling everything kept some of the proceeds for themselves and laid part at the Apostles' feet. Peter told them that they did not have to sell everything, or having sold it were not required that they give it all. But evidently they wanted people to think they had given all. Their sin was spiritual pride. Peter told them they had not lied to men but to God. The Spirit power of love and unity was so strong in the community that Ananias had a heart attack and fell over dead. The same happened to Sapphira (Acts 5:1-16).

Everyone was filled with the wonder of the living Lord and of the consciousness of His presence through this new gift of the Holy Spirit. Their commitment to the Lord included every phase of their lives.

Centuries later we walk in this same wonder of God's blessing.

THE FIRST BIG MIRACLE

Peter said, "I have no silver or gold, but I give you what I have; in the name of Jesus Christ of Nazareth, walk."

(Acts 3:1-10.)

There was a naturalness in the new power available through the Holy Spirit and an almost unconsciousness of guidance in the use of that power. It was not a self-consciousness of power, but the consciousness of Christ power through the Holy Spirit. Peter and John must have passed the lame beggar at the Beautiful Gate in Jerusalem many, many times as they went to the temple. But on this day they stopped. They had no money to give, but this time they knew they had something so much greater. They asked the man who had been lame from birth to get up and walk. He not only walked, but he went into the temple walking and leaping. No wonder he was "praising God" and not the men. How could mere men do this? All the people were astounded with wonder and amazement. Peter did not claim any new power for himself: "Why do you wonder at this, or why do you stare at us, as though by our own power or piety we had made him walk?" . . . The faith which is through Jesus had given the man this perfect health in the presence of all.

Then a new Peter showed a new kindness and compassion, "And now, brethren, I know that you acted in ignorance, as did also your rulers." Then Peter appealed to them to accept this Jesus whom the prophets had told about.

O Lord, help us to grow in this Christ consciousness so that through Thy Holy Spirit we can be used to bring glory to Thee.

FIRST OPPOSITION

And as they were speaking to the people, the priests and the
captain of the temple and the Sadducees came upon them,
annoyed because they were teaching the people and proclaiming
in Jesus the resurrection from the dead. And they arrested
them and put them in custody until the morrow, for it was
already evening. (Acts 4:1-3.)

In spite of opposition and persecution many others joined the
new Christian fellowship until the number grew to be 5000.

When the apostles were brought before the authorities after
they had been arrested, they were asked, "By what power or by
what name did you do this?" That was indeed a pertinent
question. Peter, filled with the Holy Spirit, answered, "Be it
known to you all, and to all the people of Israel, that by the name
of Jesus Christ of Nazareth, whom you crucified and whom God
raised from the dead, by him this man is standing before you well"
(Acts 4:5-31).

The authorities were now the bewildered ones. They could not
speak in opposition because the evidence of a real miracle was
before them. They cried, "What shall we do with these men?" All
they could do was to threaten Peter and John. That did not bother
Peter and John at all. They answered, "Whether it is right in the
sight of God to listen to you rather than to God, you must judge;
for we cannot but speak of what we have seen and heard."

The authorities were caught. They were professed religious
men; they were also political men and were afraid because of the
popularity of these "uneducated men" who had such influence
with the people.

The Christian friends met in a prayer meeting. They did not
pray for protection from persecution, only for courage to meet
whatever might happen as they lived this new life. No wonder the
place was shaken and they all had more infilling of the Holy Spirit.

Lord, keep us in this same consciousness of Thy presence.

THE FIRST ORGANIZATION

Now in these days when the disciples were increasing in number, the Hellenists murmured against the Hebrews because their widows were neglected in the daily distribution. The apostles called the disciples together and said, "Brethren, pick out from among you seven men of good repute, full of the Spirit and of wisdom, whom we may appoint to this duty." (Acts 6:1-15.)

The Hellenists were Jews who spoke Greek and may have come from Greek-speaking countries. They also had become Christians but had some difference in their culture from the Hebrew-speaking Jewish Christians, so they got missed in the distribution of food, especially their widows. They appointed seven men as deacons, evidently out of the Hellenist group.

I have heard modern preachers criticize the apostles because they said, "It is not right that we should give up preaching the word of God to serve tables. . . . But we will devote ourselves to prayer and to the ministry of the Word." This division of ministry displeased our modern men. They have a point, but if we read further we will find a greater truth: their openness to the guidance of the Spirit and their recognition of the work of the Spirit in breaking down organization walls. Of those seven men appointed as deacons, Stephen became the first Christian martyr after *preaching a sermon*. The deacon, Philip, became Philip, the evangelist, until the end of the story. And we have no record that any apostle ever told him, "We appointed you to deke, now you deke." What's more, later Paul visited in the home of "Philip, the evangelist" who was then living in Caesaria, and even more surprising, Philip had four daughters who prophesied. That is, they preached. And it was evidently more surprising that they were unmarried. Nowhere do we have any mention that Paul objected to these women preaching.

We need organization in the church, but we must never hinder the work and outreach of the Spirit by being bound to rules behind organization walls.

Help us to be free in the Spirit.

BREAKING DOWN RACE WALLS

For God so loved the world that he gave his only Son, that *whoever* believes in him should not perish but have eternal life.   (John 3:16.)

And Peter opened his mouth and said: "Truly I perceive that God shows no partiality, but in every nation any one who fears him and does what is right is acceptable to him."
(Acts 10:34,35.)

From Old Testament history we know the truth of Peter's statement to Cornelius, "You yourselves know how unlawful it is for a Jew to associate with or to visit any one of another nation" (Acts 10:29). It is enlightening to see how God, through the Holy Spirit, could get Peter to the place where he could say, "But God has shown me that I should not call any man common or unclean." (This wall developed because in early history the "people of God" were not strong enough to resist the inroads of idolatry; so at first it was only a protective measure, but it became a feeling of special favor in God's sight.) How could God get His love for all people across to these new Christians? Besides all that, it was taken for granted in the Christian community that no Gentile could become a Christian without first becoming a Jewish proselyte.

Israel was an occupied country. Cornelius was an officer in the occupying army, but he was "a devout man who feared God with all his household, gave alms liberally to the people, and prayed constantly to God." God heard him and sent an angel to him. The angel told him to send for one Peter who was then in Joppa. He was even given Peter's address! So Cornelius sent three men to Joppa to bring this Peter to them. Would he come? The three men would likely be concerned all the way as they walked the thirty miles to Joppa. They loved their master and did not want him to be disappointed. Just before they arrived in Joppa the Holy Spirit got Peter ready to receive these Gentiles!

We never know what God can do until we obey Him.

SPECTACULAR GUIDANCE

The next day as they were on their journey and coming near the city, Peter went up on the housetop to pray, about the sixth hour.   (Acts 10.)

Peter was hungry and while food was being prepared he prayed. (He used waiting periods for prayer.) Could he smell the food being prepared? Anyway, as he prayed he fell into a trance and he had a vision of food. A sheet was let down from heaven and in it were all kinds of animals etc. that a Jew was forbidden to eat. A voice came to Peter, "Rise Peter, kill and eat." Peter answered, "No Lord, I have never eaten anything common or unclean." This happened three times.

While Peter was inwardly perplexed, the men sent by Cornelius were at the gate asking for "Simon Peter." While Peter pondered the vision the *Spirit* said to him, "Behold, three men are looking for you. Rise and go down and accompany them without hesitation; for I have sent them."

The Spirit did not tell Peter that the three men were Gentiles! Peter would see that himself, but when he saw them he was so sure of the Spirit's guidance that he said to them at once in a most redeeming way, "I am the man you are looking for: what is the reason for your coming?" Then they told about their master and his request. For the first time in his life, Peter entertained Gentiles. He kept them as guests all night and ate with them. The next day with some other brethren from Joppa they went with the men to Caesaria. By walking they did not arrive until the next day. They found Cornelius waiting for them.

Lord, help us to live so close to Thee that we also may be ready always to receive guidance.

THE FIRST GENTILE CHRISTIANS

While Peter was saying this, the Holy Spirit fell on all who heard the word. And the believers from among the circumcised who came with Peter were amazed, because the gift of the Holy Spirit had been poured out even on the Gentiles. For they heard them speaking in tongues and extolling God. Then Peter declared, "Can anyone forbid water for baptizing these people who have received the Holy Spirit just as we have?" (Acts 10:23-48.)

Cornelius was expecting them, so great was his faith in God. So he had called in his kinsmen and his close friends. Cornelius didn't know any better yet, so when Peter arrived he fell down at his feet and worshiped him. Peter could not take this so he said, "Stand up; I too am a man."

Then Peter told about his assurance in coming and Cornelius told about his vision and action in obedience. Then Cornelius said, "Now therefore we are all here present in the sight of God, to hear all that you have been commanded by the Lord." What a setting for a witness!

Peter told of Jesus, his life and death and resurrection and of the Holy Spirit. And while Peter was still speaking, the Holy Spirit fell upon that whole group. Peter and the men with him had to accept this witness of the Spirit, so they baptized this whole group of Gentiles. Then they asked for Peter and his group to stay on with them for a few days. What a fellowship they must have had! And what an adjustment and enlargement of Peter's convictions and feelings about Gentiles! But Peter still had to report to the home church at Jerusalem. What would they think? Old culture and religious patterns had really been broken.

Help us, dear Lord, to be ready for your ideas that You want us to have.

THE HOME CHURCH ACCEPTS NEW LIGHT

The news had already reached the home church. The conservatives asked Peter, "Why did you go to uncircumcised men and eat with them?" Peter told his story and they listened. "When they heard this they were *silenced*. And they glorified God saying, "Then to the Gentiles also God has granted repentance unto life." (Acts 11:1-18.)

In every fellowship there are those who sincerely attempt to preserve the best from the past while there are others who are always ready for new ideas. This means trouble in any church unless both groups want above everything else to know God's will. And they must also listen to one another in love. This evidently happened in the first Christian church at Jerusalem. They listened to Peter and believed him when he said, "The Spirit told me to go with them without hesitation." When they heard the whole story they had no criticism to make and they glorified God because the Gentiles were also included in the promises of God.

Some years later after many Gentiles had become Christian the issue came up again. Some men came from Judea to the new Gentile churches and told the people, "Unless you are circumcised according to the law of Moses, you cannot be saved." Much debate followed and a committee had to be sent to Jerusalem to settle the question. This was the first "Annual Conference." Peter had to tell all over again how the Spirit had led in all these changes. Then he asked, "Now therefore why do you make trial of God by putting a yoke upon the neck of the disciples which neither our fathers nor we have been able to bear? But we believe that we shall be saved through the grace of the Lord Jesus, just as they will." (At that time there were 365 prohibitions, 248 commandments and 1521 Sabbath rules to be observed in the Law.)

This big meeting accepted the way of grace in the Lord Jesus and sent the message back to all the new churches among the Gentiles (Acts 15).

Lord, help us to live above the law and in the discipline of Thy grace through the Holy Spirit.

THE FIRST MISSIONARY TO THE GENTILES

Saul of Tarsus was a most unlikely candidate for a Christian missionary. He was the leading persecuter of the new Christian group. He was a missionary for Judaism and he had no mercy for any one not faithful to the law. When Stephen was stoned his garments were laid at Saul's feet, so he assented to Stephen's death (Acts 7:54 to 8:1). A great persecution broke out against the Christians. "Saul laid waste the church, and entering house after house, he dragged off men and women and committed them to prison."

But Saul, still breathing threats and murder against the disciples of the Lord, went to the high priest and asked him for letters to the synagogues at Damascus, so that if he found any belonging to the Way, men or women, he might bring them bound to Jerusalem. (Acts 9:1-22.)

All the time that Saul was persecuting the Christians he thought he was serving God. There was nothing wrong with his commitment. He just could not see that this Jesus was the Messiah that he expected with all his heart. God had to knock him down to get him. On the road to Damascus God got him.

Now as he journeyed he approached Damascus, and suddenly a light from heaven flashed about him. And he fell to the ground and heard a voice saying to him, "Saul, Saul, why do you persecute me?" And he said, "Who are you, Lord?" And he said, "I am Jesus, whom you are persecuting; but arise and enter the city, and you will be told what you are to do."

The men with Paul heard a voice but saw no one. When Saul arose he was blind and they had to lead him into the city. He was blind for three days and could not eat or drink anything. Then the Lord had to get Ananias ready to go to Saul in a vision. Ananias was hesitant because he had heard why Saul was coming to his city. But the Lord said to Ananias, "Go, for he is a chosen instrument of mine to carry my name before the Gentiles and kings and sons of Israel; for I will show him how much he must suffer for the sake of my name. So Ananias went at once, and laying his hands on Saul he said, "Brother Saul, the Lord Jesus who appeared to you . . . has sent me that you may regain your sight and be filled with the Spirit."

After Saul was baptized and took food, he immediately began to proclaim Jesus. So the greatest missionary of all time was set on his ministry.

We rejoice with the Apostle Paul, as he became known later.

PART THREE

The Gifts of the Spirit
  —In Manifestation
  —In Ministry

THE GIFT AND THE GIFTS

Now concerning spiritual gifts, brethren, I do not want you
to be uninformed.   (I Cor. 12:1.)

An Assembly of God missionary in India said to me one time,
"Always remember that on the Day of Pentecost it was the gift of
the Spirit and in Corinth the issue was on the *gifts* of the Spirit."

Saul became known by his Roman name, Paul, as he was turned
loose on the whole Roman and Greek world witnessing to the
wonder of a living Lord. His three long missionary journeys are
well known. He founded many churches, and as he travelled he
never forgot his new Christians. We are privileged to have the
letters he wrote to them. His letters to the Christians at Rome and
to the ones in the area of Ephesus give us his understanding of the
wonderful gospel of grace which he preached. His other letters
were written to specific situations and were really counselling
letters.

Paul was a superb, loving counsellor. He wrote to the Corinthians:

For though I am free from all men, I have made myself a
slave to all, *that I might win the more*. To the Jews I became
as a Jew, *in order to win Jews*; to those under the law I
became as one under the law—though not being myself
under the law—*that I might win those under the law*. To
those outside the law I became as one outside the law—not
being without law toward God but *under the* law of Christ—*that
I might win those outside the law*. To the weak I became
weak, *that I might win the weak*. I have become all things to
all men, *that I might by all means save some*. *I do it* all for the
sake of the Gospel, *that I may share in its blessings*. (I Cor.
9:19-23.)

Paul wrote to the church in Corinth as Christians "called to be
saints" for whom he gave thanks. He said they were not lacking in
any spiritual gift. Then he proceeded to talk about all the
problems they had in the church. They still had many things to
learn, hence his counselling letter. Today we call his counselling
"being involved." He began where they were and then challenged
them to new growth in Christ. This was never *compromise*; it was
counselling.

Thank you, Lord, for your loving patience with us also.

THE CHURCH AT CORINTH

For it has been reported to me by Chloe's people that there is quarrelling among you. . . . (I Cor. 1:11.) Now concerning the matters about which you wrote . . . (I Cor. 7:1.)

So Paul had an individual report about the church problems as well as a letter from the church. They were quarrelling over which preacher they liked best, Paul, Apollos or Peter, and the sanctimonious ones said, "We are the Christ party." There was arrogance, spiritual pride and even immorality among them. They had marriage problems; they were going to the civil courts with problems that should have been settled in their Christian fellowship. They still had leanings toward idol worship. They had problems with their women, the good women who became Christians with their husbands but had never had freedom before as they had in the Christian church. The spiritual value of their love feasts was ruined by their self-centeredness. Above all, they were competitive about the gifts of the Holy Spirit. (These must have been "the Christ party" . . .) So Paul wrote to them as "babes in Christ."

No one comprehends the thoughts of God except the Spirit of God. Now we have received not the spirit of the world but the Spirit which is from God. . . . The unspiritual man does not receive the gifts of the Spirit of God, for they are folly to him, and he is not able to understand them because they are spiritually discerned. (I Cor. 10-16.)

Corinth was a Roman city in the midst of Greece. Throughout all Europe and the Middle East it was an insult to call any man a Corinthian because of the recognition of the wickedness of this city. How could Paul have expected a Christian church there? This is only the measure of his faith in the power of the Holy Spirit.

Before Paul came, this city was very religious. They had temples in their city to eight pagan gods. In relation to the later problems in the new church there, I suppose the temples of most interest to us would be the one to Asklepius, the god of healing, and the one to Aphrodite, the goddess of love. Her temple housed 1000 priestesses who were really religious prostitutes.

It seems that the biggest difficulty in the new church was not being religious, but being religious in the name of Christ. Were they a cult or in the real family of God?

We, today, must learn this important lesson. Guide us, Lord.

A CHRIST-CENTERED EXPERIENCE

You know that when you were heathen, you were led astray
to dumb idols, however you may have been moved. Therefore
I want you to understand that no one speaking by the Spirit of
God ever says, "Jesus be cursed!" And no one can say "Jesus
is Lord" except by the Holy Spirit.   (I Cor. 12:1-3.)

Paul's first test of the authenticity of a religious experience as
being from God was: "Is it Christ-centered?" Jesus had said on the
night before His death as He told about the coming of the Spirit,
"When the Counselor comes, whom I shall sent to you from the
Father, even the Spirit of truth, who proceeds from the Father,
he will *bear witness to me.*"

The experiences and all ecstacy in the pagan religions were
manipulated. I have seen the manipulation for experience among
Hindus and Moslems. This was very true in all of Greece and
Rome. Paul was not arguing for any one gift of the Spirit. His only
question was, "Whatever gift of the Spirit you have, *is it given to
you or did you manipulate to get it?*" In the experience itself it is
hard sometimes to know the difference. But Paul gave tests for the
authenticity of any experience of any gift of the Spirit. And the
first test is, "Is it Christ-centered?"

Paul also saw the possibility of manipulating an experience by
good works, even in the name of Christ (Gal. 3:1-5). We never
earn God's gift or His gifts. They are indeed *gifts.*

Boasting and conflict always follow a manipulated gift. This had
become true in the Corinthian church. In boasting each one said
his gift of the Spirit was the best one. This is why they were in
conflict. They were centering on their own individual experiences
instead of centering on Christ. We cannot get together or stay
together except as we make Christ central. He is our experience.
In Him we have unity and not conflict.

*O Lord, help us always to know when we get away from
Thee.*

VARIETIES OF GIFTS

Now there are varieties of gifts, but the same Spirit; and there are varieties of service, but the same Lord; and there are varieties of working, but it is the same God who inspires them all in every one. (I Cor. 12:4-6.) All these are inspired by one and same Spirit who apportions to each one individually as he wills. (I Cor. 12:11.)

Paul insists that there is no reason for conflict because of differences in gifts. He said the church body is like our individual bodies. Every body consists of different parts. The foot cannot say the hand is not a part of the body. Nor can any other part of the body say it is the whole body. Paul pleads for no discord in the body because of differences. "If one member suffers, all suffer together; if one member is honored, all rejoice together" (I Cor. 12:26).

Then Paul makes his definite plea:

Now you are the body of Christ and individually members of it. And God has appointed in the church first apostles, second prophets, third teachers, then workers of miracles, then healers, helpers, administrators, speakers in various kinds of tongues. Are all apostles? Are all prophets? Are all teachers? Do all work miracles? Do all possess gifts of healing? Do all speak with tongues? Do all interpret? (I Cor. 12:27-31.)

The inference from the questions is that there are truly varieties of gifts.

O Lord, keep us humble toward one another so that we can be united in Christ, no matter how we differ.

BLEST TO BE A BLESSING

To each is given the manifestation of the Spirit for the common good.   (I Cor. 12:7.)

Since you are eager for the manifestations of the Spirit, strive to excel in building up the church.   (I Cor. 14:12.)

God never gives any one a special gift of the Spirit just for his own good. God's concern is for every one. He blesses each of us to be used of Him to reach others whom He also loves.

It is so easy to be lost in a new experience of the Lord that we want to hug the experience. If we do that, we will forget the Lord. It is easy, too, to want to be with those of like experience of the Spirit; then we make others feel left out. Some of the ones who may feel left out may be the very ones hungry for a new experience of the Lord, and by our arrogance we have pushed them away. When any one receives the "baptism of the Spirit" his family should receive the first benefit of the new experience. Any blessing given to any one of us is given for the common good. Any one in a local church who receives a new gift and blessing from God is given it to be a blessing to that church. The "colder" the church may be, the more the blessing is needed for all. If we seek fellowship only with those of like experience and faith we are set to become a cult.

We live in a generation when great emphasis is placed in our secular world upon *feeling* and *experience*. If we are not careful, we might be responding to our secular culture instead of our Lord who gave His life for our salvation.

Any new experience of the Lord only deepens our relationship to Him. It is the relation that is important, and not our *feeling* at any time.

Lord, keep us in the center of Thy will and use us as Thou seest fit.

THE LOVE TEST

And I will show you a more excellent way. If I speak in the tongues of men and of angels, but have not love, I am a noisy gong or a clanging cymbal. And if I have prophetic powers, and understand all mysteries and all knowledge, and if I have faith, so as to remove mountains, but have not love, I am nothing. If I give away all I have, and if I deliver my body to be burned, but have not love, I gain nothing.

(I Cor. 12:31-13:3.)

Love is the movement of the Spirit, and without love any amount of commitment and giving, any kind of religious experience is of no value. Since God is love, to be like Him we must also have this same love. We cannot make ourselves love, but this love is part of the gift of the Spirit. Paul gives the interpretation of this love:

Love is patient and kind;
Love is not jealous or boastful;
it is not arrogant or rude.

Love does not insist on its own way;
it is not irritable or resentful;
it does not rejoice at wrong,
but rejoices in the right.

Love bears all things,
believes all things,
hopes all things,
endures all things.

Love never ends.
Prophecy, tongues, knowledge will pass away,
but love endures.
So faith, hope, love abide, these three;
but the greatest of these is love.

(I Cor. 13.)

Make love your aim.

TONGUES: GIFT OR MANIPULATION?

I thank God that I speak in tongues more than you all;
nevertheless, in church I would rather speak five words with
my mind, in order to instruct others, than ten thousand
words in a tongue. (I Cor. 14:18,19.)

An Assembly of God missionary in India said that Paul's tongue
experience was the same as he spoke in Romans 8:26: "Likewise
the Spirit helps us in our weakness; for we do not know how to
pray as we ought, but the Spirit himself intercedes for us with
sighs too deep for words." In our day this is called the prayer
language.

The Corinthians knew about tongues-speaking and how to
manipulate it. Victor Duruy in THE WORLD OF THE GREEKS
(Minerva S.A., Geneva, 1971.) describes such an experience. The
priest was the interpreter, which was known as the oracle of
Delphi. Paul had only one question, "Was your experience
manipulated or did God give it to you?"

After a lesson in California on the Holy Spirit, a written
question was handed to me. It was: "Do you go along with
coaching people in voicing syllables to help them receive the
tongues?" That was easy to answer. I said, "That is pagan." We
had a very dear friend in India whose first warm experience of the
Spirit was with Pentecostal people. He received the gift of
tongues and was God's gift to the Assembly of God. They really
listened when he spoke. I went to hear him in Chicago. He said to
those Pentecostal people, "If you seek tongues you'll never find
the Lord. Seek the Lord and take whatever He gives you."

I have no argument for or against tongues. I have no hang-ups. I
have heard the manipulated kind which really sounds pagan. I
know when the Holy Spirit came to me and took me out of
agonizing self effort. The peace and new relationship was so
dynamic that I have never needed tongues nor any other demon-
stration. The disciples needed something special on the Day of
Pentecost. It took a like experience for Peter with Cornelius to
know that Cornelius was already accepted of the Lord without first
becoming a Jew.

*We want Thee only, and we trust Thy Holy Spirit. We take
whatever gift Thou dost desire to give us.*

SPIRITUAL MATURITY

Brethren, do not be children in your thinking; be babes in evil, but in thinking be mature.   (I Cor. 14:20.)

What then brethren? When you come together, each one has a hymn, a lesson, a revelation, a tongue, or an interpretation. *Let all things* be done for edification. If any speak in a tongue, let there be only two or at most three, and each in turn; and let one interpret. But if there is no one to interpret, let each of them keep silence in church and speak to himself and to God. Let two or three prophets speak, and let the others weigh what is said. If a revelation is made to another sitting by, let the first be silent. For you can all prophesy one by one, so that all may learn and all be encouraged; and the spirits of the prophets are subject to prophets. For God is not a God of confusion but of peace.   (I Cor. 14:26-33.)

In other words, Paul is saying that all public services of the church should be orderly. This is to say that the closer to God one is, even in ecstasy, the freer the human will is. Even though the experiences of tongues and prophecy are gifts, still they can be controlled by the human will. This was in opposition to pagan ecstatic experiences in which people got to the place that they did not know what they were doing.

It is interesting that it was in this context that Paul spoke of women being silent in church. They must have become arrogant with their new Christian freedom, since Paul had to say to them: "What! Did the word of God originate with you, or are you the only ones it has reached?"

God limited Himself in creation by giving man the right of choice. Our choosers must be trained. God never overrides the human will. But we do have the responsibility of choice, even our choice of God and the reception of His gift of the Holy Spirit.

Help me, O Lord, to exercise mature choices.

THE MINISTRY GIFTS

And his gifts were that some should be apostles, some prophets, some evangelists, some pastors and teachers, for the equipment of the saints, for the work of the ministry, for building up the body of Christ. (Eph. 4:11-12.)

This gift of ministry is more than a personal aptitude and talent test shows; it is a gift that provides new energy to any natural gift. The Spirit-gifted person will serve in such a way that people will recognize a power greater than natural gift or training. This is when God is praised.

Our human difficulty is that too many in "God's service" have served in their own natural strength and have not been available for extra power through the Holy Spirit.

Some one said that that is like pushing a Cadillac up a mountain. What a relief that we do not need to do God's work in our own strength!

Beyond energizing a natural gift, some have been given gifts of ministry beyond any dream. Bakht Singh of India is an illustration. Naturally, he was exceedingly shy and his voice was an enlarged whisper. After his conversion he felt called to preach the good news. He said to the Lord, "If you want me to preach you'll have to give me courage and a voice." Several years later I was with him in a national youth conference in India. His strong voice reached a thousand people without a microphone.

God can surprise you if you let Him.

THE PURPOSE OF MINISTRY

Until we all attain to the unity of the faith and the knowledge of the Son of God to mature manhood, to the measure of the stature of the fulness of Christ; so that we may no longer be children tossed to and fro and carried about with every wind of doctrine, by the cunning of men, by their craftiness in deceitful wiles. Rather, speaking the truth in love, we are to grow up in every way into him who is the head, into Christ from whom the whole body, joined and knit together by every joint with which it is supplied, when each part is working properly makes bodily growth and upbuilds itself in love. (Eph. 4:13-16.)

We all grow together. That is the church. Our unity is in Christ and we grow to be like Him. If we keep growing in Him we cannot be fooled by all the crafty men who want to manipulate us. We are together only as we each keep our own connection with the Lord.

Keep us in this loving growth!

PART FOUR

*The Fruit of the Spirit
and
New Life for Growth*

NEW LIFE

If any one is in Christ, he is a new creation; the old is passed away. Behold the new has come. (II Cor. 5:28.)

It is Good News that no matter what kind of life any one has lived there is always this offer from God to start all over again with a clean page. The past can be fully cleansed. Jesus called this being "born again." Some religious people are still going on human effort and need to be born again. Jesus even told a theologian that he needed to be born again (John 3:-15). Being born again is to be born into the family of God. A preacher in India said in a Bible class, "I have a temper. I can't help it. My father had a temper. I inherited it from him." I asked, "Which father are you talking about? Your earthly father or your heavenly Father?"

We must accept a clean break with the old life. Paul wrote to the Colossians:

And you, who once were estranged and hostile in mind, doing evil deeds, he has now reconciled in his body of flesh by his death, in order to present you *holy and blameless and irreproachable* before him. . . . (Col. 1:21,22.)

It is amazing how many people carry a sense of guilt, even church members. One woman said, "I know God forgave me but I can't forgive myself." I asked her if she thinks she is better than God.

Christian living is not "getting away from it all"; it is not merely ignoring life's problems. It is bringing them into the presence of a loving heavenly Father who can take away all guilt. An old hymn says, "He breaks the power of cancelled sin." This is the healing of all memories.

You can bring anything to the God of love. He is waiting for you.

BEING BORN AGAIN IS NOT ENOUGH

... holy and blameless and irreproachable before him,
provided that you continue in the faith, stable and steadfast
not shifting from the hope of the gospel which you heard.
(Col. 1:22,23.)

The Apostle Paul desired that every one become *mature* in
Christ. Paul recognized that the Corinthian Christians were still
"babes in Christ," so he had much patience with them, but
wanted them to grow. Some people seem to think that when they
were "saved" they were finished—that they had arrived. The fact
is that they had just started. The steadfastness in Christ will keep
one growing more like Him. Some think that after a new
experience of the Spirit they have arrived! No, this is just a new
start with fuller life.

—building up the body of Christ, until we all attain to the
unity of the faith and of the knowledge of the Son of God, to
mature manhood.

We are to grow up in every way into him who is the head, into
Christ, from whom the whole body, joined and knit together by
every joint with which it is supplied, when each part is working
properly, makes bodily growth and upbuilds itself in love (Eph.
4:12-16).

We are members of God's family now and we must grow
together in love.

In your meditation, think of God's loving patience. Remember
that growth is possible because of the Holy Spirit which is the
growing power. And, He is within you.

THE SECRET OF SPIRITUAL PROGRESS

But you shall receive power when the Holy Spirit has come upon you; and you shall be my witnesses. . . .   (Acts 1:8.)

Too much of our witnessing and our church work has been done in our own human strength. Human efforts alone bring us into a deep sense of futility. The promise of the Holy Spirit is not only for abundant life but for fruitful service. Peter said, "For if these things are yours (meaning divine power) and abound, they keep you from being ineffective or unfruitful. . . ." (II Peter 1:3-11).

Since this power is a *given* power, we must be careful not to go ahead of what God wants for us. This is why we need much silence before Him. We must have patience to wait for His time. At the beginning of His ministry Jesus waited forty days until He was sure of the Father's guidance.

Jesus had not told the disciples about the need of future organization. He did not tell them exactly how to baptize. He did not even tell them that the day would come when Gentiles could become Christians without first becoming Jews. This was probably the greatest upheaval in all church history. But as individuals and as a church they stayed open to God's guidance in their service to Him, and in due time they learned.

Praise God that we don't have to do His work in our own strength.

WALK IN LOVE

Walk in love, as Christ loved us and gave himself up for us, a fragrant offering and sacrifice to God. (Eph. 5:2.)

God-love is not a feeling word. It is not an experience I feel, but an action I live. It is a giving love. God so loved the world that He gave His son (John 3:16). Our love for God is measured by our love for one another. "Beloved, if God so loved us, we ought to love one another" (I John 4:11).

It is true, we often *feel* unloving to those with whom we live and work. That is exactly the time to do some loving thing for them. We may be too tired to *feel*, but someone else may be in great need of love. It also helps to think of others as God sees them. We must see them through Christ's eyes. Anyway, this kind of love is a gift, and we will be helpless until we look to Him and accept His gift of love for those who may be irritating us. The *feeling of love* is always a bonus resulting from the *act of love*.

For your meditation read I Cor. 13:4-7.
You need not despair if you find too little love in your life.
Just accept the gift, the God-love waiting for you.

51

WALK IN LIGHT

Now you are light in the Lord; walk as children of light.
(Eph. 5:8.)

Jesus said, "I am the light of the world; he who follows me
will not walk in darkness, but will have the light of life."
(John 8:12.)

The pesky thing is that "light is capable of 'showing up' everything for what it really is" (Eph. 5:13, Phillips). One early morning
in Landour, India, I was coming down the mountain when I met a
little woman climbing up the path. She stopped me and said, "I'm
so glad to see you. I prayed for you this morning and God gave me
a special message for you. It is, 'Whenever we *see* that we have
failed in anything, it is evidence that we are walking in the light,
or we would not see it.' " This is one of the most practical things I
have ever learned in my Christian life. This dear woman did not
know that I had been kicking myself because I kept seeing areas in
my life where I had not grown. What a joy it was to know that
seeing any failure was evidence that I was walking in the light.
From that day, forty-three years ago, I have not wasted any
energy kicking myself. I can add that God will not give me a vision
at night to tell me where I am failing if my husband already knows.
He will tell me through my husband. I thank God for revealing
failure so that I can continue to grow.

I found a plaque which I put up in the kitchen for my good
husband to see. It says, "Please be patient—God isn't finished
with me yet." God isn't finished with any of us yet, but He can
continue His work in our lives if we continue every moment in our
commitment to Him.

In your meditation thank God for the light of His love.
What does His light reveal to you that needs to be exposed to
His love?

THE SPIRIT BEARS FRUIT

The fruit of the Spirit is love. . . .   (Gal. 5:22.)

It takes time for fruit to grow.   (John 15:16.)

God *is* love. He loves us because of what He is and not according to what we are. If He lives in me I will grow in love. All my reactions to others will be determined by that God-love and not by what others do to me. Paul spoke of his unworthiness as an apostle and then said, "It is through the love of God that I am what I am, and the love which he showed me has not been wasted" (I Cor. 15:10, 20th century).

Evelyn Underhill, the perceptive English Christian mystic, realized this:

Quite early in the life of prayer we often begin feeling an exultant delight in God; religion seems full of love, joy and peace. And then that same spirit of love begins the relentless penetrating and transforming of our ordinary life; and things are not so nice. Life asks many distasteful tasks from us, shows us many inconvenient opportunities of love. . . .

(Fruits of the Spirit, page 9.)

These inconvenient opportunities for love are our opportunities for real growth in Christian life. They really test the quality of our love.

Can you find inspiration in your meditation time in thinking of people who are hard to love? You can if you think first of God's love for you—and for all those unlovely people.

This love is not only a fruit, but a gift.

MORE FRUIT

The fruit of the Spirit is love, *joy*. . . .   (Gal. 5:22.)

The first response to an experience of God's love is an inexpressible sense of joy. New Christians bubble over with this unprecedented sense of joy. They are like the honeymoon couple who said to me, "No one ever loved like we love." But it wasn't six months until the bride called me long distance at midnight! What she called joy and love had melted away in the heat of an argument. Had she lost her joy? Yes, only as far as she was depending only on feeling.

Real joy is a fruit of the Spirit, not a gratification of one's emotions. It is God-centered and other-centered. It never depends on circumstances. When the Apostle Paul wrote to the Philippians, "Rejoice in the Lord always; again I say rejoice," he was in jail for his belief in Jesus as the Messiah. Real joy is praise to God under any circumstances, because God will give strength to meet anything. That is why Paul could be full of joy even in prison.

There is a great difference between this joy and what the world calls happiness or pleasure. This joy comes from relationship with God, a relationship so deep through the Spirit that is in our very inner being. Because it is so deep, it is unaffected by the superficial and momentary affairs of life. This joy is mentioned 150 times in the New Testament. Knowing of his coming death the next day, Jesus said to his disciples, "So you have sorrow now, but I will see you again and your hearts will rejoice, and no one will take your joy from you (John 16:22).

Rejoice!

THERE'S MORE!

The fruit of the Spirit is love, joy, *peace*. . . .

(Gal. 5:22.)

Peace that is fruit of the Spirit is not mere absence of conflict or war. It is not a static calm. It is very dynamic and powerful.

On the last night before his death Jesus told his disciples, "Peace I leave with you; my peace I give to you; not as the world gives do I give to you (John 14:27)." And this Jesus could say when He knew He was going to be murdered the next day. This is peace indeed. We were created to have relationship with God. So real peace is found in doing his will. Peace and deep joy as well as love are permanent characteristics of the one in whose inner being the Spirit finds an abiding place.

Paul said that Jesus is our peace (Eph. 2:14). He did not learn that in a quiet place all by himself with His God; he learned it out in a cruel world that made life very hard for him. It was a dynamic, sustaining peace that took him through conflicts, hazards, persecution, and made it possible for Him to rejoice in the Lord always.

This peace is also a gift as well as a fruit of the Spirit. It is yours for the acceptance of Jesus who is our peace.

AND MORE FRUIT

The fruit of the Spirit is *love, joy, peace, patience, kindness, goodness, faithfulness, gentleness*. . . .   (Gal. 5:22.)

Patience, kindness, goodness, faithfulness, gentleness were all qualities Paul never had before he accepted Jesus as his Messiah. He knew they did not come through self-effort.

Patience: There is a Dutch saying, "The hurrier I go the behinder I get." I keep that in my kitchen also. Common sense tells us this is true. Only love, and the love of God at that, makes real patience possible. Sometimes irresponsible people are thought of as being patient, especially by themselves. That is not patience; it is simply not caring.

Kindness: An impatient person cannot be kind. Kindness is love in action. A self-centered person is kind only when he gets some return from it. Since God is patient and kind to everyone, it is through the gift of His abiding presence in one's inner being that love can be manifested in real kindness.

Goodness: This means that all pious masks are discarded and love with all its concommitant qualities is authentic all the way through one's life. When superficial old patterns of action sometimes reappear there is enough integrity to confess and change at once.

Faithfulness: "continuing in the faith, stable and steadfast, not shifting from the hope of the gospel" (Col. 1:23).

Gentleness: Before his conversion, how rough Paul was with those he thought to be in the wrong! He had no mercy for those whom he considered unorthodox (Acts 8:4-8). He did all this in the name of God! Then the risen Lord found him on the Damascus road. Read all the Corinthian letters to see how gentle he became, even with Christians so slow to learn.

As you meditate on this fruit, do not be discouraged. Just remember that His Spirit is the growing power.

UNDER LOVE CONTROL

The fruit of the Spirit is love, joy, patience, kindness, goodness, faithfulness, gentleness, *self-control*.   (Gal. 5:22.)

In the secular world it is taken for granted that every one has
hurts and hates. The only thing they know to do is to push the ugly
feelings down into the inner being and get ulcers or to spit them
out and lose friends. This is not surprising, but when a minister of
the Good News takes this approach in a sensitivity group I am
surprised.

In Christ we have another answer. We can be under the control
of the love of Christ. "For the love of Christ controls us" (II Cor.
5:14). We can be a new creation with a new disposition more like
our new heavenly Father. Coming into God's family can be an
instant experience, but growing up in God's family to maturity
takes time.

For a long time I thought Paul was strange in ending this list of
the fruits of the Spirit with *self-control*. This sounded too much
like getting back to self and to self-effort. Then I found the
meaning of the Greek word translated *self-control*. It is not the
"dynamite" word for power but another word which we have in
demo-*cracy*. That is "people power," but here it is *power* with the
prefix *put in*. This means that for a Christian, self-control is really
Christ-control put in by the Holy Spirit into the inner being.

So we go back to God-love which is the first fruit of the Spirit
and look to Christ for strength to accept His love in any situation.
Any good feeling is a result of love action and a wonderful bonus.

This can all lead to deep meditation.

THE PROBLEM OF SELF

If any man would come after me, let him deny himself and take up his cross daily and follow me. (Luke 9:23.)

In the summer of 1958 a beautiful 22-year-old American girl flew to Ceylon to become a Buddhist nun. She sacrificed her long hair, her comfortable life, her fiancé and her medical studies. She said, "I've been convinced that only through Buddhism can I find true happiness." Referring to her fiancé she said, "I gave him up because I realize that marriage and love are selfish." She thought she had to give up all human love in order to give her life to God. She did not know that God's love is not like the bird that pushes the other bird out of the nest. God's love never pushes other loves out; it sanctifies human love and makes it an illustration of God-love. Through Christ, love for God and human love are not only compatible; they are one and the same quality of love.

It is so often forgotten that the same Jesus who talked about giving up self also said, "I came that they may have life and have it more abundantly" (John 10:10).

Buddha came to the conclusion that all suffering was due to *desire*. So the only way he saw to find peace was to get rid of all desire. This is often called a "non-self" condition.

In all religious history, including Christian, many earnest seekers have been led into asceticism. They think that to get rid of self is to do without comforts and to bring about suffering. They "mortify the flesh." This can become as self-centered as any other type of arrogance.

O Lord, help us to know what You meant by giving up self.

THE REAL SELF

No man can serve two masters; for he will either hate the one and love the other, or he will be devoted to the one and despise the other. (Matt. 6:24.)

There is even a perfume that must have been named for half-dedicated Christians. It is called *Slightly Wicked*. These are the ones who try to be only halfway good while clinging to some of their old ways. This is psychologically impossible, to say nothing of the spiritual impossibility. Inner conflict is devastating.

Dr. Karen Horney's discernment has been an enormous help to me: "The real self is the alive, unique center of ourselves: the only part that can or wants to grow." (*Neurosis and Human Growth*, page 155.) She says the pseudo-self is the whole pride system which may have developed within us and which is really egocentricity. Dr. Fritz Kunkel called egocentricity "condensed darkness." Everything that leads to true fulfillment is in the real self. Everything in the pride system is destructive. We must always face the fact that the pride system can work in religious terms as well as any other. It was not Jews as such who killed Jesus; it was religious self-interest and pride of position.

As Christians we affirm the real self and deny only the false self. In these words Jesus' teaching is that we should deny our false self and then we can find the abundant life He promised.

O Lord, help me to say "yes" to Thee and "no" to all that is not like Thee.

WHO AM I?

Whoever would save his life would lose it, but whoever loses his life for my sake will find it.   (Matt. 16:25.)

For over a decade people have been asking the question, "Who am I?" But they never seem to find the answer. It is like going around on a merry-go-round and getting off where you got on. They are looking in the wrong place to find their own identity.

Those who demand the *right* of self identity seem to stand out in competition with everyone. They seem to be in rebellion against society and all people in it. They seem to say, "I am a person. You'd better recognize me."

In speaking of those who are ultimately victimized by their own unfulfillment, Dr. Loomis said:

"There are ways of coming to know oneself that do not require lasting preoccupation with the self. There are ways of believing in oneself without making oneself the center of the universe. There are ways of accepting oneself without rejecting others. . . . While we may have to sacrifice far more or less than we dream, in the process of coming to know and accept ourselves for what we are, we often fear most the loss of illusions rather than the true giving up of the self. (*The Self in Pilgrimage*, pages 9, 10.)

Jesus said that preoccupation with one's own self is not the way to self-realization or self-fulfillment. This is true, not merely because Jesus said it. He said it because He knew it was a law of human personality development.

Self-centeredness, indeed, leads only to condensed darkness.

Help us, O Lord, not to be afraid to give ourselves to Thee and to others.

FINDING MY REAL SELF

Whoever loses his life for my sake will find it.—Jesus

In putting others first there often comes the fear that this will lead to nonentity or non-self. This is an illusory fear. Peter wrote to new Christians, "Once you were no people but now you are God's people" (I Peter 2:10). The safest thing is to put God first because He wants only our fullest self-realization, which is life abundant.

The British economist, Barbara Ward, saw this. She said:

Every single ancient wisdom and religion will tell you, don't live entirely for yourself, live for other people. Think what it means in concrete terms. Don't get stuck inside your own ego, because it will become a prison in no time flat—and for God's sake don't think that 'self-realization' will make you happy. That is the way you will end in hell—your own hell. . . . True self-realization comes in going out to others, to creation, to art, to knowledge. One of the oldest truths is that he who loses his life will find it. (McCall's Magazine, June 1967.)

Evidently the law of putting others first works in any case, but it is even more potent when we begin by putting God first and then others next. Knowing that God loves me and calls me by name helps me to love others for whom He does the same. His love helps me to love myself without being afraid of the darkness of self-centeredness. So I am free to be myself without hurting others.

Thank you, God, for creating me like this—to be loved of Thee and to be able to love all others.

A POSITIVE EXPERIENCE

Indeed I count everything as loss because of the surpassing
worth of knowing Christ Jesus my Lord. For his sake I have
suffered the loss of all things and count them as refuse, in
order that I may gain Christ and be found in him.—Paul
(Phil. 3:8.)

Paul's emphasis was not on what he had given up but on what
he had received. It wasn't a sinful life or even one of pleasure that
Paul had given up; it was a very religious life, but one of self-
effort. He gave up all the possibilities which the future held for
him as a result of his excellent training. He gave up family,
prestige, honor and even power. He gave up all the things the
world counts good. Even these good things he counted as garbage
compared to what he found in Christ. No wonder his emphasis
was on what he received and not on what he gave up.

Jesus asked the rich young ruler to give up his wealth, not
because money is bad but because it was first in his life (Matt.
19:16-22). Anything other than God that becomes first in our lives
is idolatry. Even if it is good it should not come before God. We
are created to put God first.

Of course, common sense tells us that "sin" is bad for us. The
writer of Hebrews said it is a weight: "Let us lay aside every
weight and sin which clings so closely, and let us run with
perseverance the race that is set before us, looking to Jesus the
pioneer and perfecter of our faith" (Heb. 12:1,2).

I wonder if at times we have not overemphasized what must be
given up, because we have not adequately emphasized the love of
God in our Lord Jesus Christ.

O Lord, we come and give everything to Thee.

DISCARD THE NEGATIVES

You have died, and your life is hid with Christ in God. . . .
Put to death therefore what is earthly in you: immorality,
impurity, passion, evil desire, and covetousness, which is
idolatry.   (Col. 3:3-5.)

Immorality, impurity, passion are all from results of desecrated
sex which is one of God's great gifts to man. It is *evil desire* that is
wrong. The ability to desire is God's gift to us so that we can have
the motivation to desire Him and all He has for us. Covetousness
is the result and curse of self-centeredness. the strange thing is
that our western economy is set up on the basis of covetousness:
this year your refrigerator must be bronze, you are odd if you
don't have a color TV etc.

Then Paul gave the Colossians another list of things to get rid of:
anger, wrath, malice, slander, dishonesty and lying, "seeing that
you have put off the old nature with its practices and have put on
the new nature, which is being renewed in knowledge after the
image of its creator" (Col. 3:5-10). How often anger and wrath are
defended by "good" people! It is "righteous anger" or "we are still
human." Of course, we are still human. It is the defense of such
lack of control that is the real sin. And slander—that is gossip! If
we had a moratorium on gossip in our church groups for six
months, miracles would happen.

Why are we afraid to embrace our virtues? Basically we resist
recognition of our assets because, once recognized, they must
be *used*. For goodness makes claims. It must be expressed. It
must be used. Otherwise, it becomes evil in our hands.
Badness is goodness damned up. (Earl Loomis in *The Self in
Pilgrimage*, page 6.)

Set us free, Lord, so that we may be renewed every day.

THE NEED OF A NEW WARDROBE

Put on then, as God's chosen ones, holy and beloved, compassion, kindness, lowliness, meekness, and patience, forbearing
one another, and if one has a complaint against another,
forgiving each other; as the Lord has forgiven you, so you also
must forgive. And above all these put on love, which binds
everything together in perfect harmony.   (Col. 3:12-14.)

It is very special to be a chosen people. Once Paul would have
thought this privilege belonged only to the Jews. Then as now, too
often it is forgotten that God chooses all people to be a blessing to
all people. Paul wrote this to former Gentiles who were now
Christians. Peter also said it beautifully:

But you are a chosen race, a royal priesthood, a holy nation,
God's own people, that you may declare the wonderful deeds
of him who called you out of darkness into his marvelous
light. Once you were no people but now you are God's
people; once you had not received mercy but now you have
received mercy. (I Peter 2:9,10.)

This is why we need a new wardrobe—we are going somewhere
on a mission.
Today I am going to a wedding. I want to be dressed properly to
show respect and love for my friends. Also, when clothes are worn
out I do not cling to them; it is a relief to dispose of them. Our
whole attention is on the new wardrobe which is appropriate to
wear on the mission to which we are called.

*Dear Lord, help me to count as refuse all things that would
hinder me as a chosen person to represent Thee.*

THE NEW CLOTHES

The new "clothes" that we are to put on are all virtues that have to do with human relationships. We must face the fact that our relationship to God is always tested by our relationship to all other people, especially to those nearest us.

These new clothes are for the inner being, but they will show on the outside. There can be no self-conscious pretense of love. The change must be from the inside out. It is a new nature possible because of what Paul called "Christ in me."

Compassion, kindness and *patience* are qualities that give others new courage and dignity. I've just about come to the conclusion that the greatest gift we can give to children, family, to anyone, is new courage for life and for being their best selves. This is what Jesus does for us. It is what we as His followers should do for others.

Lowliness takes us out of the competitive market. Lowliness is not the false humility that depreciates oneself and is always talking about being "humble." It is never *self*-conscious. It is *Christ*-conscious and *other*-conscious. Real humility never cringes. False humility is really arrogance in reverse.

Meekness is never weakness. It is real strength. One stands tallest in true dignity when he is free enough to put the welfare of others beyond his own interests. This is the reason it becomes easy to forgive, because we understand others in their situations. We understand not only others but also God's love for them as well as for ourselves.

The binding force in all of this is love. His love makes the new clothes possible. Thank you, Lord.

RESPONSIBILITY OF CHOICE

Solid food is for the mature, for those who have their faculties
trained by practice to distinguish good from evil.

(Heb. 5:14.)

For freedom Christ has set us free; stand fast therefore, and
do not submit to a yoke of slavery. (Gal. 5:1.)

A slave is one who cannot help himself or make his own choices.
Christ has set us free so that we can have the ability to make
choices. Tagore, the wise Indian poet and educator, saw this great
truth. He said, "I am able to love my God because He gives me
freedom to deny Him." (*Fireflies*, page 157.)

If then you have been raised with Christ,
seek the things that are above,
Set your mind on things above.
Put to death therefore what is earthly in you,
Put on then . . .

After those choices which I must make, Paul adds:

Let the peace of Christ rule in your hearts;
Let the word of Christ dwell in you richly
as you serve and praise. (Col. 3:1-7.)

Christ's part is to give the peace but we have to choose His way
and accept the peace. God's word dwells in us and grows as we use
it for others. ". . . as you teach and admonish one another in all
wisdom." A thankful heart is an open heart, never hard and
closed. ". . . as you sing psalms and hymns and spiritual songs with
thankfulness in your hearts to God."
So we are free to "do everything in the name of the Lord Jesus
giving thanks to God the Father through him."

*Dear Lord, this day I renew my covenant with Thee, to live it
Thy way. Thank you for making this possible.*

HUMAN RELATIONSHIP

Be subject to one another out of reverence for Christ.
(Eph. 5:21.)

When relationship to another person is called "being subject" to that person, it really hits hard. No one wants to be anyone's doormat. The fact is that there is nothing in all the Bible which says that anyone is to be another person's doormat. The great American fear is that of being "walked over." The door for such subjection is too often opened by misinterpretation of scripture, especially when the verb is translated as "submit."

So what does it mean to be "subject to another?" The Greek verb translated "be subject to" or in King James "submit" means "to arrange under" or "to put yourself under." The important thing in this is that a choice is implied. It does not mean "take anything that happens to you." It is not passive, docile resignation; it is not cringing self-effacement or mere complaisance. It is choosing the best welfare of the other one. It is really putting the other one first. When a woman lets her husband treat her cruelly she is hurting him more than she is being hurt. In all relationships this is true. Letting people get by with the misuse of power is more detrimental to the one misusing the power. We have had too many instances of this in families and in the political world.

The way to fulfillment is away from the darkness of self-centeredness by putting the best welfare of others first. The fear then often comes, "Where do I come in?" Remember, Jesus said, "Love your neighbor as yourself." That means you do love yourself first because you are first of all responsible for yourself. Therefore, you must do what is best for yourself. That you find by doing things for others.

Lord, this is hard to see. Give us light—and courage.

THE SOURCE OF AUTHORITY

There is no reverence of Christ in worship unless there is real reverence in the heart. If reverence is in the heart for Christ, it will show in relation to all persons.

Be subject to one another out of reverence for Christ (Eph. 5:21). We do not have two areas in our hearts for our relationships—one for God and another for other persons. We act according to what we are in the depths of our being. No person, man or woman, can be humble and reverent toward God and then act or feel arrogantly toward any human being.

So the ability to love and respect another person depends upon our relationship to God. This is the reason that true fulfillment comes first of all out of one's commitment to God. Because of this God relationship we can see all people as God sees them. Paul said, "The love of Christ controls us. . . . therefore, we regard no one from a human point of view" (II Cor. 5:14,16).

We usually call this having respect for one another. Even children need to be respected. When we see God's love for every individual it is also easier to have respect for ourselves.

It helps to understand a "bossy" person when we remember that such "bossiness" is the result of an inner insecurity and that "bossiness" is only false authority. It is a substitute for the real thing. Real authority begins with reverence for the Lord who loves every person. This authority is the use of power that is for the benefit of others and never *over* them.

Open our eyes, Lord, to the authority of Thy love.

WIVES AND HUSBANDS

Wives, submit yourselves to your husbands as to the Lord.
(Eph. 5:22.)

This is one of the most misinterpreted verses in Scripture. The verb is not even repeated in the original Greek, and this is only a participial phrase added on to verse 21. The verb is in the previous verse where it is given as a law for *all* human relationships. Whatever basic attitude is required for a wife toward her husband is also, therefore, required of a man in all his relationships.

I think the Apostle Paul applied this statement to wives first because he thought that women who were created to be mothers would be the first to understand what quality of life he was talking about.

Many Christian wives are told they must keep up their husbands' ego. Does this mean she will make him more self-centered? If so, she is hurting him spiritually. I say, keep up his *courage*, not his *ego!*

I know some Christian women who have been told they must "obey" even non-Christian husbands because a woman must obey a man! That is easy to answer if he asks her to do something wrong because the relationship is to be "in the Lord." There is no difficulty in the woman-man relationship if both are truly committed to the Lord.

To respect one another means to think of the other's best welfare. (See Eph. 5:33.) This closest of human relationships is indeed a mystery.

Lord, help us to live Thy love in this closest of relationships.

A HUSBAND'S AUTHORITY

For the husband is the head of the wife as Christ is the head
of the church, his body, and is himself its Savior.

(Eph. 5:23.)

Many Bible people talk about the "order of command": God,
Christ, man, woman. I have no objection to the order, but the use
of the word *command* is not Christ-thinking. Especially as it is
usually defined in this instance. Paul also said, "There is neither
slave nor free, there is neither male nor female; for you are all one
Christ" (Gal. 3:28). To the Corinthians, in answer to pagan
Grecian ideas about the marriage relationship, he said, "For the
wife does not rule over her own body but the husband does;
likewise the husband does not rule over his own body but the wife
does" (I Cor. 7:4). Paul made them partners. Aristotle, 300 years
before Paul, said that man is superior and woman is inferior, that
man was made to rule and woman to be ruled. It is particularly
relevant that in that social context Paul made them partners.

Then man's headship is described as the same as Christ's
headship. And Jesus said He did not come to be ministered unto,
but to minister (Matt. 20:27,28, KJV). He also said, "Whosoever
would be great among you must be your servant" (Matt. 20:26). So
European theologians in 1952 came to the conclusion that a
husband is the head of his wife when he is her servant!

Authority for the Christian is power *for* the benefit of others
and never *power over them*. If we can find this secret in the
closest human relationship, we will be able to live it in all of life.

Lord, help us to know the servanthood of Jesus without fear.

HEADSHIP DEFINED IN LOVE

Husbands, love your wives as Christ loved the church and gave himself up for her, that he might sanctify her, having cleansed her by the washing of water with the word, that the church might be presented before him in splendor, without spot or wrinkle or any such thing, that she might be holy and without blemish. Even so husbands should love their wives as their own bodies. He who loves his wife loves himself. . . . For this reason a man shall leave his father and mother and be joined to his wife and the two shall become one. This is a great mystery . . .   (Eph. 5:25-33.)

If a husband loves his wife as Christ loves the church she will have no difficulty whatever in being subject to him or in putting his welfare first. He cares for her and she cares for him. Only in such a partner-relationship can either be free. Neither one is ever subjected to the selfish will of the other. Neither one has to be defensive of his or her best welfare. Each one sets the other free to be his or her best self. One may love opera and the other sports, but that need never break the mystery of a wonderful relationship.

The Greek word for "love" of a husband to his wife is not a sex word but the "agape" word, which is a cherishing love, an action word. This goes back to the main verb of Paul's sentence (vs. 18-22) which is, "Be filled with the Spirit." The great mystery of this relationship is possible to those who accept God love as a gift. Each one is reverent toward Christ so each is spontaneously reverent toward one another. Frankly, I think Paul added with a smile, "However let each one of you love his wife as himself, and let the wife see that she respects her husband" (5:33).

Lord, help me to be responsive to Thy love so that I can truly love my husband and all others.

FREEDOM UNDER ANY CIRCUMSTANCES

For freedom Christ has set us free; stand fast therefore, and do not submit again to a yoke of slavery. (Gal. 5:1.)

Many women today who are caught in unhappy circumstances are made to feel great anger in consciousness-raising groups. The anger is understandable but hardly the most Christian way out of any dilemma.

It is often forgotten that freedom begins in one's inner being. Dr. Viktor E. Frankl said he discovered in a Nazi concentration camp that "the last of human freedoms is the ability to choose one's attitude in a given set of circumstances." (Page xiii, *Man's Search For Meaning*.)

The Apostle Paul said: "This priceless treasure we hold, so to speak, in a common earthenware jar—to show that the splendid power of it belongs to God and not to us. We are handicapped on all sides but we are never frustrated; we are puzzled but never in despair. We are persecuted, but we never have to stand it alone; we may be knocked down but we are never knocked out!" (II Cor. 4:7-9, Phillips).

So, for a Christian, the first step out of oppression is not anger, but inner freedom.

O Lord, help us to walk with dignity through any circumstances that may overwhelm us and lead us on from here in any way that we can witness to Thy love.

THE REAL SLAVERY

Someone said, "There is no one so much a slave as the person who had his own way all his life."

Love does not insist on its own way.   (I Cor. 13:5.)

For the love of Christ controls us, because we are convinced that one has died for all: therefore all have died. And he died for all, that those who live might live no longer for themselves but for him who for their sake died and was raised.

(II Cor. 5:14,15.)

Sometimes it seems to me that the American refrain is, "I can't help it." People are imprisoned by their own negative feelings and unhappy circumstances. They can't find their way to freedom because they are always thinking about themselves only. Self-pity is always a prison.

The way out of the prison of self-centeredness is first of all to put God first in one's life. This is where the Holy Spirit makes it possible. It is not only getting away from life's griefs but it is bringing them to the God of love. He always helps us understand others, and He clarifies our circumstances so that we can find our way out or through.

God, first of all gives peace, which is the beginning of freedom in any circumstance, and then He gives us the understanding of love. Many times such love has led to the salvation of the troublemakers.

O Lord, keep us free from the curse of self-centeredness.

PRAYER IS A RELATIONSHIP EXPERIENCE

The disciples of Jesus were praying men but they saw something in the prayer life of their Lord which was different. So they asked him to teach them to pray. He gave them the prayer which begins, "Our Father." It begins with relationship and it begins with God, the Father, not with our human needs.

In the Luke account (Luke 11:1-13) Jesus gave the people a parable of the friend at midnight. This "friend" was an *unwilling giver*. Then Jesus told about the father who was a *willing giver* in meeting his child's needs. But the heavenly Father is the *most gracious giver*. If a human father will give good gifts to his son, *"how much more* will the heavenly Father give the Holy Spirit to those who ask Him?" The Holy Spirit is the supreme gift from the Father because this is the giving of Himself to each one who comes to Him. This is the most anyone can ask. And He gives graciously.

Sometimes we may be unwise in what we ask. I am thankful some of my requests were not given to me. But we come to Him knowing always that He knows best for each one of us. We come with the assurance that He always answers us even though He may not grant a specific request. Any child knows that "No" is just as much of an answer as "Yes."

Because He is my Father, I never need to beg. An answer to my prayer is not my right; it is always a special boon. God is so good.

He is my heavenly Father; therefore I am His Child.

GOD MY HEAVENLY FATHER

Our Father who art in heaven. (Matt. 6:9.)

And yet, he is so near: *"filled with all the fulness of God,"* through His Spirit in the inner man. Christ *dwelling in my heart by faith."* (Eph. 3:16-19.)

But this God is also the creator of all the earth and of all that there is. He is so great and still so approachable. He is within and without. What there is of Him within me makes it possible for me to have communication with the great Creator of the universe.

O Lord, our Lord,
    how majestic is thy name in all the earth!

When I look at thy heavens, the work of thy fingers,
    the moon and the stars which thou hast established;
What is man that thou art mindful of him,
    and the son of man that thou dost care for him?

Yet thou hast made him little less than God,
    and dost crown him with glory and honor.
Thou hast given him dominion over the works of thy hands;
    thou has put all things under his feet,
all sheep and oxen, and also the beasts of the field,
    the birds of the air, and the fish of the sea,
whatever passes along the paths of the sea.
    O Lord, our Lord,
how majestic is thy name in all the earth. (Ps. 8.)

Our Father who art in Heaven, We worship Thee, who art also so near.

HALLOWED BE THY NAME

Reverence is a rare experience in our modern culture. Even in our churches it is too often thought of as a feeling. Worship committees plan how to create a "worship atmosphere." Such "worship" lasts as long as the "atmosphere" does not change. To hallow the name of our Father is more than a matter of sentiment, feeling, or mood.

To hallow God's name is to recognize the fullness of His character. Before Jesus, the justice of God was realized. Jesus revealed the fullness of God's love. God cares. He cares for everyone, even the sinner. That is why He sent Jesus. Jesus lived that love. And Jesus did not leave us desolate. He sent the Holy Spirit of God for each of us.

Even though the love of Jesus be not deserved, still He loves. No person is ever lost in the crowd so far as our Father God is concerned.

When we see the greatness of God and then the love shown in His Fatherhood, we cannot help but worship. It is a spontaneous response to hallow His name.

Were the whole world of nature mine,
That were a present far too small;
Love so amazing, so divine,
Demands my soul, my life, my all.

—*Isaac Watts*

THY KINGDOM COME, THY WILL BE DONE
ON EARTH AS IT IS IN HEAVEN

I do not believe Jesus would ask us to pray this prayer to taunt us. So he must have meant that we pray it seriously for our own nation, our own city, and our own homes. If we take this seriously we must know what it means.

I remember a cartoon from years ago. A man gave little Ferdinand a new watch. He was so delighted he walked down the street looking at his watch. Then he came to the town clock. The time did not match his watch. So he got a ladder and climbed up to change the town clock to match his little watch. This is the way many people pray. They want to make God do it as *they* see it. Without question, God wants the best for every one of us. But we must always remember that in creation He limited Himself by giving man the responsibility of choice. God never invades any person's will. We must choose His will, learning to know how He thinks, and cooperate with His will. Often we need to use the patience which is a gift of the Spirit.

In any circumstance, we must always remember that *God is always faithful*.

May Thy will be done, Lord.

GIVE US THIS DAY OUR DAILY BREAD

God is our heavenly Father, the creator and sustainer of life. He will meet every present need if we look to Him. Some people are so "spiritual" that they will not pray about everyday needs.

At a retreat one summer Dr. John Biegeleisen was leading a seminar on prayer. Dr. Beigeleisen had been trained to be a rabbi. The risen Lord got him very much as He got the Apostle Paul. He became a New Testament teacher and scholar. In the seminar he made the statement that "God knows all my needs. I don't have to tell Him." The next day a young minister said to him, "Brother John (as we called him), I couldn't sleep last night. Do you mean to say you don't pray about things?" Brother John answered, "Oh, God is my heavenly Father. I talk everything over with Him." He meant that even though he didn't need to, he was free to tell God anything.

When we see God as our Father who cares, we come to Him with any details of daily life that are a concern.

A Swiss minister coming through Nazi Germany stopped to call on friends. The husband had been taken at night by Hitler. The wife did not know where he was. When she went to the grocery store she would not raise her arm to say "Heil Hitler" so sometimes they would not sell to her. Her children were under-nourished; they did not have enough to eat. Still they prayed the Lord's prayer. The minister asked, "How can you pray 'Give us daily bread' when your children are starving before your eyes?" She said, "We don't have to live. We need only to be faithful."

O Lord, help us to know the proper relationship of all material things to the things of Thy kingdom.

FORGIVE US OUR DEBTS AS WE ALSO
HAVE FORGIVEN OUR DEBTORS

God is not bargaining with us—"You forgive and then I will forgive you." God forgives. That is His nature. He is real love. But the fact is that if my heart is hard toward anyone it is closed also toward God and He cannot get in. There is only one love area in my heart. So my forgiving relationship with others is the determining factor in my reception of the forgiveness of God. This is the bridge over which every Christian must pass. The secret of power in prayer lies right here.

Conscientious Christians often ask about the unpardonable sin. The first answer to all such concerned people is that if you have concern, you haven't committed it. The only sin God cannot forgive is the one when there is no longer any concern. When that is the case, there is no ability to receive forgiveness. It is not God's fault. It is because of a dead conscience.

The ability to love and forgive is hardly human nature. This love is a gift from God just as His forgiveness is a gift. No matter how helpless we are concerning our feelings and reactions, we need only to come to Him and He will hear us.

Praise God for such love. And believe it exists, remembering that His love exists because He lives. God is love.

FORGIVENESS IN ACTION

If your brother sins against you, go and tell him his fault, between you and him alone. If he listens to you, *you have gained your brother*. (Matt. 18:15-22.)

Jesus thought of this situation. He told us what to do if someone sins against us. You are to go to him to win him as a brother and not to "tell him off."

If he does not listen to you, take one or two others with you and try again. Then if he still will not listen, tell it to the church. You do not bring him to the church to prove him a sinner but to win him in love. If he won't listen even to the church, "let him be to you as a Gentile and a tax collector." In my youth I saw many people put out of the church at this stage, counted as a contaminating influence. Then one day I read that Jesus said, "For I came not to call the righteous but the sinners" (Matt. 9:13). He said this when He was criticized for eating with sinners.

Actually, instead of turning one's back on the "sinner" one must begin all over again. There is nothing left now but to pray.

Truly, I say to you, whatever you bind on earth shall be bound in heaven . . . Again, I say to you, if two of you agree on earth about anything they ask, it will be done for them by my Father in heaven. For where two or three are gathered in my name there am I in the midst of them. (Matt. 18:22,23.)

I wonder if these two or three are not the ones you took along to help to win your brother or sister. Peter knew that Jesus was still talking about forgiveness. He said he was willing to forgive seven times when legally three times was the limit. Jesus said seventy times seven, which meant forgiving forever.

Forgive us as we have forgiven, Lord.

LEAD US NOT INTO TEMPTATION

The Greek word for *temptation* is often translated *test* or *trial*. Since Jesus used this word, we should take His meaning of temptation. Look at His temptation experience (Matt. 4:1-11). He did not flirt with temptation. He had only one desire in life which was to do the Father's will. The assurance of His Father's pleasure in Him had come at His baptism. He had had a growing intuition that the prevalent theological interpretations of the ministry of the expected Messiah were not correct. Surely God's kingdom was more than geographical; its aim was more than to save Israel from Rome. It must be to save His people from sin. The struggle was so intense that He did not even hunger for forty days.

Then *after* forty days light broke through the fog of His humanity and He *knew*. He would never buy followers with food or any physical appeal. He would never catch them with mere propaganda. He would not use the world's methods to get followers. The only issue for Him had been "What is the Father's will?" As soon as the issue was clear, He knew the answers (Matt. 4:1-11).

We go forth with the prayer, "Thy kingdom come, Thy will be done." The matter of commitment was settled from the beginning. The only creditable temptation for a Christian comes in the time area when he is not sure of God's will. This is a time to hold to naked faith, knowing that God will eventually guide.

Lead us not into temptation. Enable us to be willing not to flirt with it.

DELIVER US FROM EVIL

In a day when there is so much permissiveness of all kinds of "sin" it is strange that there is so much talk about the devil. Not only talk but movies, one after the other, have a theme about the devil.

Some ministers seem to talk more about the devil than about the Lord. "Do you want to scare people into the kingdom?" I said to one minister, "I am not afraid of the devil because Jesus has already conquered him." Jesus said the devil had no power over Him. If I accept Christ in me I need not be fearful either, just wise enough never to be fooled. He does not come in a red suit with horns on his head and a fork in his hand. If he did, we would quickly rebuff him.

We can be insulated against this adversary of God. Paul wrote:

Finally be strong in the Lord and in the strength of his might. Put on the whole armor of God, that you may be able to stand against the wiles of the devil. For we are not contending against flesh and blood, but against the principalities, against the powers, against the world rulers of this present darkness, against the spiritual hosts of wickedness in the heavenly places. Therefore take the whole armor of God, that you may be able to withstand in the evil day, and having done all to stand.

After Paul lists the components of the Christian armor he adds:

Pray at all times in the Spirit, with all prayer and supplication. To that end keep alert with all perseverance. . . . (Eph. 6:10-20.)

When we pray "deliver us from evil," we can expect an answer to our prayer. Believe it.

FOR THINE IS THE KINGDOM AND THE POWER AND THE GLORY FOREVER. AMEN.

The church added this word of praise to the prayer Jesus gave His disciples. It is much like the prayer King David prayed in preparation for the building of a temple to the Lord.

Blessed art thou, O Lord. . . . Thine, O Lord, is the greatness, and the power, and the glory, and the victory and the majesty. . . . In thy hand are power and might; and in thy hand it is to make great and to give strength to all. And now we thank thee, our God, and praise thy glorious name. (I Chron. 29:10-13.)

The disciples had asked for a lesson on prayer from their teacher. As children we were proud when we learned to say it. As we grew up, too often we have merely *said it*. It is not only a prayer to be repeated often, it is a pattern for one's whole life. It begins with the relationship we may have with a heavenly Father who loves us and cares for our welfare even more than we can care. To Him we commit our all, knowing we can trust Him. We recognize that He is interested in every phase of our lives here on earth. We may talk everything over with Him. He will not baby feed us; we have our part to do in life, for this is a child-Father relationship. Also, we are not His only children. So no matter what happens we must always remember that He is always faithful. To remain open to receive His love and mercy we must also be open to others, even to those who do us harm. No matter what trials and tests come, we abide in His love and wait until guidance becomes clear.

We praise Thee, Lord, because we can be Thy children and members of Thy great family. And that we can wait for Thee.

PRAYER FOR HEALING

Is any among you sick? Let him call for the elders of the church, and let them pray over him, anointing him with oil in the name of the Lord; and the prayer of faith will save the sick man, and the Lord will raise him up; and if he has committed sins, he will be forgiven.   (James 5:13-16.)

I know many people who were healed through the prayer of faith, but I know many others who were not healed. I know three terminal cancer patients who were healed after prayer, but my only brother died of cancer. The whole church prayed for him; still he left us. However, for anyone who loved the Lord as he did, death was victory and not tragedy. It is not ours to ask why, only to be faithful.

In any case the faith is *in the Lord* and not in any man's words of prayer. I am sure that the greatest prayer is, "In any case may God be praised." And I would say that if any suffering of mine can be used for His glory I will gladly suffer. An American minister, through a tragedy in Europe, landed in a hospital there. The surgeon who operated on him had lost faith in God during the Hitler days. This patient was the means of spiritual healing to his doctor. God can use all circumstances if we let Him (Rom. 8:28).

There is a humanly contrived faith which is closely related to religious pride. This happens so easily to those who have had some success in healing prayer. As one minister said to a patient, "I have faith that you will get well; if you don't, it is your fault, not mine." (This is a crime against a sick person.)

There is a faith that is given by God. When that faith is *given*, the prayer for healing is effortless, and only God is praised.

We are Thine, O Lord, no matter what!

ALL THESE DISEASES

If he has committed sins, he will be forgiven.

(James 5:15.)

Some diseases are physical only. Even those are often healed. Jesus healed many such diseases, so did His disciples after the day of Pentecost. There are also many diseases now called psychosomatic. They develop because of destructive attitudes. Anxiety, worry, hate are all causes for sickness. There isn't even any use in praying for a person's body if that person has unforgiveness in his heart toward anyone. If there is any harbored guilt about anything that happened in the past, that must also be cared for first. This is called the prayer for healing of the memories.

Any healing of the spirit is even more of a miracle than healing of the body. to all such it can easily be said, "Your faith has healed you." One minister crippled by polio once said at a banquet, "I thank God my soul is not crippled like my body." His crutches, which never gave him self-pity, had been a great witness for God's healing power, for this man has had a very valuable ministry. His spirit is whole, even though his body is not.

The hymn line, "He breaks the power of cancelled sin," is a freedom shout. No matter what has happened to anyone in the past, freedom can come instantly because of the grace and love of God, if that grace is accepted. God cannot push his love down our throats because He limited Himself in creation by giving humans the responsibility of choice.

Thank you, Lord, for this love and grace.

GIVEN POWER IS FOR SERVICE

But thanks be to God, who in Christ leads us in triumph, and through us spreads the fragrance of the knowledge of him everywhere. For we are the aroma of Christ to God among those who are being saved. . . . Who is sufficient for these things? For we are not, like so many, peddlers of God's word; but as men of sincerity, as commissioned by God, in the sight of God we speak in Christ. (II Cor. 2:14-17.)

If we go out in our ministry in our own strength we are peddlers and mere salesmen for ourselves. Paul added to the Corinthians' letter: "Not that we are sufficient of ourselves to claim anything as coming from us; our sufficiency is from God, who has qualified us to be ministers of a new covenant, not in a written code but in the Spirit; for the written code kills, but the Spirit gives life" (II Cor. 3:4-6). In all Paul's ministry among the Gentiles he was hounded by "Christians" who still really lived under the old law, the old covenant. They didn't realize that Jesus had brought a new covenant. Paul was brokenhearted many times because they followed him around the country and confused the new converts to Christ.

We still have the same problems in many churches from people with the same legalistic attitude. They always cause division even among conscientious Christians. Even the New Covenant, the New Testament, can be followed legalistically. This legalistic approach is an arrogant human approach and is not of the Spirit.

O Lord, keep us in Thy love as we represent Thee—free in the Spirit.

GOD'S LOVE FOR THE WORLD

Jesus prayed for His disciples: "I do not pray that thou shouldst take them out of the world, even as I am not of the world, but that thou shouldst keep them from the evil one. They are not of the world, even as I am not of the world. Sanctify them in the truth; thy word is truth. As thou didst send me into the world, so I have sent them into the world." (John 17:15-18.)

This is too often pictured as the Christian turning his back on the people of the world when it is only on the evil of the world. Jesus loved sinners without ever condoning the sin. The Apostle Paul saw this distinction.

Therefore, if anyone is in Christ he is a new creation; the old has passed away, behold, the new has come. All this is from God, who through Christ reconciled us to himself and gave us the ministry of reconciliation; that is, God was in Christ reconciling the world to himself, not counting their trespasses against them, and entrusting to us the message of reconciliation. So we are ambassadors for Christ, God making his appeal through us. (II Cor. 5:17-20.)

The astounding part of this statement is that God does not count the sins of the world against the sinners. Karl Barth, in his early years, said, "It is not our sins that separate us from God but our unwillingness to have them forgiven." Actually God is not against us for our sins: He is with us against our sins. We have to learn that lesson for ourselves before we go out with condemnation for those who do not know the Lord.

Lord, help me truly to represent Thee to all the people who do not know Thee. If I meditate on that simple sounding prayer for ten minutes, more lives than my own will be changed.

OUR WITNESS MISSION

You shall receive power when the Holy Spirit has come upon you; and you shall be my witnesses in Jerusalem and in all Judea and Samaria and to the end of the earth.   (Acts 1:8.)

When we think of witnessing, we think of *telling* what the Lord has done for us, often whether people want to hear it or not. If we talk about missions, people think first of foreign missions. It is easy to *talk* and it is easy to think of a *foreign* mission. It is a different matter when we begin at home where the family and the community know if we are consistent or not. Living the witness is the hardest witnessing, but that's where the power starts which makes all the rest fruitful.

Peter had a message for wives whose husbands had not yet come to the Lord:

Likewise, you wives, be submissive to your husbands, so that some, though they do not obey the word, may be *won without a word* by the behavior of their wives. (I Peter 3:1.)

This is the hardest witnessing, the living of it. For the comfort of modern women, the verb for *submissive* is the same one used in Ephesians 5:21 and 22. It means to *put yourself under* the best welfare of the other one. It has no implication that any woman should obey anything that is wrong because her man demands it. It is an outgoing verb and not a doormat idea. Mahatma Gandhi called this the rose theory of witnessing.

Jesus got people *ready* to hear and then He told them His message. Once in a while the attack method is what is needed, but it is wise to be guided by the Holy Spirit because only He knows when that method counts.

Jesus said, "When I am lifted up I will *draw* all men to myself" (John 12:32).

Give us wisdom, Lord, truly to witness for Thee. Select a difficult situation or person right now and meditate on what Jesus might do—how He might feel about that person or situation. What do you feel? How do you plan to handle it? If His way seems impossible, remember that "you shall receive power!"

WITNESS BY LIFE STYLE

But seek first his kingdom and his righteousness; and all these things shall be yours as well. (Matt. 6:33.)

The intellectual, yet childlike Quaker philosopher, Thomas Kelley, wrote: "Simplicity is ordered complexity." Think for a minute on that. Then, think of the millions of young people who, back in the Sixties, began to rebel at what they saw as needless artificiality in adults both in and out of the church. In the church, they saw lives not consistent with religious profession. In the world around them, they saw the same kind of artificiality. Young people rebelled, most commonly by adopting what appeared to their elders to be wild haircuts and outlandish dress. Parents were dismayed, to say the least. But this rebellion must be taken as a challenge. Jesus understands this kind of rebellion and cuts through to reality:

Do not be anxious about your life, what you shall eat or what you shall drink, nor about your body, what you shall put on. Is not life more than food, and the body more than clothing? (Matt. 6:25.)

I often wonder what young Prince Siddartha, better known as Buddha, would have done and believed had he lived in Jesus' time. I think he would have responded to Jesus with his whole heart! Many young people today have reacted as Buddha did, because adults have not represented Jesus as He really is. The young find identity and their concept of peace by merely ridding themselves of anxiety through rebellion. Jesus has a more fruitful answer: "Seek ye first the kingdom of God—and all these things shall be added," including the abundant life which both young and old seek. Our young people still seek *simplicity* and authenticity. If we and they start with the first priority, then all things "shall be added," shall fall into place.

Think on the ordered complexity of simplicity.

THE SIMPLE LIFE

Meditate for a moment. What does the simple life really mean? To Paul, the simple life was first of all—Christ as priority. This is the way Paul wrote it:

Indeed I count everything as loss because of the surpassing worth of knowing Christ Jesus as my Lord. For His sake I have suffered the loss of all things, and count them as refuse, in order that I may gain Christ and be found in him. (Read Philippians 3:4-16.)

Paul counted material possessions as refuse in comparison to having Christ, but Jesus said possessions may be added. It has been a temptation all through church history for devout people to become ascetic, to deprive themselves. They think that doing without is the secret. Doesn't this make "things" important, but in a negative sense? Many sincere young people have now gone back to primitive living. There is nothing wrong with this, surely, but is there any real virtue in doing without modern comforts?

My husband and I started housekeeping in the Virginia mountains in a log cabin, five rooms and a bath, a spring below the house, and we didn't mind because that was what was available in our mountain mission. In all our years in India, we never had running water in the house. But none of that made us holier, and today I don't feel guilty at all with my modern conveniences. I now even have an automatic washer and dryer! I'm freer than ever to serve God because of them, and my commitment to God is deeper than ever. I thank Him for all that has been "added." Lack of things does not make us holy. Lack of them does not necessarily make us simple. Belonging to Christ, who simplifies, is the only way to the simple life.

Who, or what, is in charge of my life?

SIMPLICITY IS NOT . . .

When we do not keep Christ central, our human tendency is to go to extremes. Asceticism has always been one of those extremes for religious people. Some ascetics even go so far as body mutilation to attain spiritual merit. It is not surprising when those who think religious merit must be earned fall into this custom. But for Christians, who are supposed to know about the unmerited grace of God, it is strange. Paul had to write this to the Colossians: "Let no one disqualify you, insisting on self abasement" (Col. 2:18). In the Corinthian church some had accepted Greek asceticism and avoided all sex in marriage. Paul spoke against such ways in marriage (I Cor. 7:3). So, simplicity is not asceticism.

Simplicity is not poverty as an end in itself. It is not money that is wrong but the love of it (I Tim. 6:10). Mahatma Gandhi chose poverty as a principle in his life style. He was of a country that thought it was righteous to give up all luxuries and even comforts. But his dear friend, Mrs. Naidu (poet and governor) said that no one knew how much it cost his friends to keep him in poverty. They did it gladly because they loved him.

Too often in our country there are Christians who choose poverty as an end in itself. Actually they are living off their friends. They call it living by faith and they can make their friends feel uncomfortable if they "do not fork over." This is irresponsible faith. However, there are those who are called to live by faith, even in financial matters, but when called, they *never* make their friends feel uncomfortable.

Keep us, Lord, in the center of Thy will. And truly simple.

LEGALISM, FALSE SECURITY

Our trust always is to be in the Lord. He must be central in our lives. Whenever we begin to put other things first, we are sure to fall into legalism. This may even be holding to real truth but doing it with rigidity and not with love. One can be theologically correct in a rigid way and thus have no love of God. One can be faithful in attendance at all the meetings of the church and still be spiritually unorthodox. Even the prophets of the Old Testament saw this. Amos spoke for the Lord:

I hate, I despise your feasts,
I take no delight on your solemn assemblies . . . But let justice roll down like waters
and righteousness like an everflowing stream. (Amos 5:21-24.)

Paul had the same concern for the Galatian Christians. He wrote to them:

I am astonished that you are so quickly deserting him who called you in the grace of Christ and turning to a different gospel—not that there is another gospel, but there are some who trouble you and want to pervert the gospel of Christ. (Gal. 1:6,7.)

Paul had an understanding of the grace of God which freed him from all the old Pharisaic interpretations of the law. Through the Holy Spirit he had learned exactly what of the Jewish faith carried through into the life which Jesus instituted.

There is a security in just doing things in a certain way but it may be false security. This is falling back into immature religion. Mature religion is to be free, the freedom for which Christ set us free (Gal. 5:1).

Meditate on Gal. 5:1-7. Ask yourself where your freedom in Christ may be limited.

FREEDOM IS NOT LICENSE

For you were called to freedom, brethren; only do not use your freedom as an opportunity for the flesh, but through love be servants of one another.   (Gal. 5:13.)

All things are lawful for me, but not all things are helpful. All things are lawful for me, but I will not be enslaved by anything.   (I Cor. 5:12-20.)

To the Galatians the question was in reference to theological interpretations of the Jewish faith and what should change in following Christ. In Corinth the question of freedom was related to sexual liberty. This door was opened because in the past the Corinthians had considered sex with religious prostitutes as worship, so their consciences had to be re-trained. Also, there was the Greek idea that the body is one thing and the spirit another. So why should sexual freedom affect even a new spiritual relationship to Christ: "Sex was a physical hunger and should therefore be satisfied." (Sounds like modern America!)

It was hard for new Christians to learn the full meaning of freedom in Christ. As long as it meant only freedom from the old ways of life they would be hard and legalistic. If their freedom meant license (anything will be acceptable) it would not be freedom in Christ.

When Thomas Merton could study Eastern faiths and meditation methods because he was secure in his Christian faith, he was truly free in Christ.

As long as we can say "No" with dignity to worldly license, we are free. The secret is that we are free to be servants of one another in love.

The question I face is, "Am I free or compulsive in following Christ?"

FREEDOM IN CHRIST IS A LOVE DISCIPLINE

For the love of Christ controls us. (II Cor. 5:14.)

To Jesus, prayer and meditation were so important because they were based on His love relationship with the Father. This avoids all the "shoulds" of legalism. Under the law, people prayed as they *should*. They went to the temple as they *should*. They fasted not only as they *should*, but because they wanted everyone to know how righteous they were (Matt. 6:5,6). Jesus' life was permeated with meditation and prayer. He was free in obedience to the Father's will because of this love relationship. He *wanted* to be in constant contact with the Father.

I remember when I prayed because I knew I should—I often timed myself. Perhaps I needed that discipline at that stage in my Christian life. But thank God, I no longer take special time with the Lord because I ought to, but because I want to.

Twenty minutes of quiet in the morning and another twenty minutes in the evening! That's all right if that is all you want—just a little time of peace to be able to face life. But so much more is available if you accept the love of God and through His Spirit (God within) spend not only forty minutes but a lifetime with Him.

You do not need to "leave" God's presence when this meditation is over. In fact, you can't leave His presence if you try!

FREEDOM IS A NEW DISCIPLINE

One thing I do, forgetting what lies behind and straining forward to what lies ahead, I press on toward the goal for the prize of the upward call of God in Christ Jesus.

(Phil. 2:13,14.)

This was Paul's discipline since he had found freedom in Christ. We will miss what he meant by "straining" unless we remember that he lived in the midst of the popularity of Grecian games. This is the discipline of the athlete who is free because he is disciplined. It is the freedom of the pianist who, from disciplined hours of practice, is amazingly free on the keyboard.

To the Corinthians, Paul wrote:

By the grace of God I am what I am and his grace toward me was not in vain. (I Cor. 15:10.)

The 20th Century translation says "was *not wasted*." When we do not fully accept the grace of God, we are wasting it. A grace gift is undeserved, and it is ours only through acceptance.

In August 1966 I received a letter from New York saying that I had been awarded a magazine's free trip for two to Europe for 30 days. I found out later they put all the renewals that came that spring into a box and picked one out. My prejudiced friends said I deserved it. But if I deserved that trip I also deserved the theft of my suitcase in the Union Station in Washington, D. C., later. If it works for gifts, it also works for thefts.

My daughter, Lois, and I had just returned three weeks before from a Mideast trip, so our passports were in order. When my husband did not want to go, our Lois was delighted to go. Our time was set for the following June. We both thought some gimmick must be involved. But no, the first week in June a large envelope came—air mail, insured, registered. It contained all the tickets, a book of vouchers for taxis, extra trips, and luxury hotels plus a big check. All this promise of a trip, but the trip was not ours *until we took it*. For 30 days I felt under the miracle of God's grace.

The gift had been offered me, but I had to enter in. Meditate on the fact that blessings are ours only when we take them. Does it require a kind of discipline to receive grace? It does. Discipline and humility.

WE CAN LEARN FROM MARTHA

(Read Luke 10:37-42 and John 11:17-28.)

There are two stories in the Bible about Martha and Mary. Martha was a fussy hostess. "She was distracted with much serving," and complained to Jesus about her sister who sat at His feet and listened to His teaching. Jesus rebuked Martha for her anxiety and praised Mary for her interest in spiritual things. That must have been hard for Martha to take.

The next story takes place after their brother Lazarus had died. They had sent for Jesus but He did not arrive until four days after the burial. According to oriental custom, friends had come to mourn with the sisters. Mary was with them. She was still *sitting*. It was not Mary but Martha who heard when Jesus was coming. It was Martha who went out to meet Jesus. It was to Martha that Jesus said, "I am the resurrection and the life." The greatest evidence of spiritual change in Martha was her attitude to her sister. After she had stated her faith in Christ she went and called her sister Mary and said *quietly:* "The Teacher is here, and is calling for you." If it had been the old Martha she would have said, "If you're so spiritual, woman, don't you know the Teacher is here?" But now, out of a new quietness in her own life, she could speak quietly to her sister without reproof.

When a responsible activist learns also to be quiet, a real change takes place.

PART FIVE

Questions That Trouble People

WHY ARE THERE DISSENSIONS ABOUT THE HOLY SPIRIT?

Then let us no more pass judgment on one another, but rather decide never to put a stumbling block or hindrance in the way of a brother. (Rom. 14:13.)

We should be able to grow in love enough so that our differences of opinion would never become dissensions. Dissensions about how or when the fullness of the Spirit comes are bewildering to honest seekers. An expectation that all experiences be more alike takes the attention of seekers of Christ. Our culture demands a "high" in experience; Christ asks for an experience of *Him* through the Holy Spirit.

Paul insisted there were varieties of gifts. When we put any one first we give evidence of not trusting the work of the Spirit.

Let us join Paul in his stand:

"For I have decided to know nothing among you except Jesus Christ and him crucified. (I Cor. 2:2.)

If we do that we can trust the Holy Spirit to do His work.

IS IT A "SECOND BLESSING?"

By this we know that we abide in him and he in us, because
he has given us of his own Spirit.   (I John 4:13.)

For Peter on the day of Pentecost it was a second blessing. For
Saul (Paul) the baptism with water and the baptism with the Spirit
must have come at the same time because he was ready for both at
the same time.

I see no need to make a doctrine of the timing. Two factors
seem very important. The baptism with the Spirit on the day of
Pentecost came because they were not ready for this infilling of
power before. Jesus had to come first so they would know how to
use God power (John 7:39).

Since the day of Pentecost, it seems to me, the power infilling
depends upon maturity in obedience and a readiness to come to
an end of self-effort and then to accept fully the grace of God for
daily life.

Fixed doctrines of timing often bewilder people. The point
is—to be completely committed to the Lord Jesus.

We want all Jesus has to give us.

HOW CAN I RECEIVE THE BAPTISM WITH THE SPIRIT?

And Peter said to them, "Repent and be baptized every one of you in the name of Jesus Christ for the forgiveness of your sins; and you shall receive the gift of the Holy Spirit. For the promise is to you and to your children and to all that are far off, everyone whom the Lord our God calls to him."

(Acts 2:38,39.)

1. Jesus promised this gift and He is faithful. The gift waits to be to be accepted.
2. Complete commitment to Him is necessary in order to receive the gift.
3. The glory of the gift belongs to the Giver.
4. God knows when we are ready.
5. He respects every individual personality and need. No one copies another's experience.
6. The gift is for new growth, ministry and for a witness to our Lord.

He is faithful!

CAN I LOSE IT?

And I am sure that he who began a good work in you will bring it to completion at the day of Jesus Christ.

(Phil. 1:5.)

So often when people have a deep experience of Christ (a Jesus "high"!) they cannot understand the "letdown" which follows. This never means a real loss unless we take back our commitment to the Lord. It is only an emotional rest period and another lesson in faith.

A real experience of Christ through the Holy Spirit is more than emotion. It is relationship. Only I can break that relationship. Jesus will never break it.

I learned a parable on the Mediterranian Sea in 1930. We came home from India on a freight boat. This ship had three motors. On a clear day we could go full speed on the power of one motor. In a severe storm it took all the power of three motors to keep us standing still. There was no progress to report in the log book. But the "progress" was that we did not land on the rocks of North Africa over to the left.

Then I realized that in times of stress and conflict, with no emotion of joy, we may be using three times as much Holy Spirit power as we do when we sing "Hallelujah."

In such times I just reconfirm my commitment to the Lord and go on. It is not long until the feeling of joy and love return.

Thank God for abiding relationship with Him through His Holy Spirit.

HOW CAN I HOLD OUT?

His divine power has granted to us all things that pertain to life and godliness, through the knowledge of him who called us to his own glory and excellence, by which he has granted to us his precious and very great promises, that through these you may escape from the corruption that is in the world because of passion, and become *partakers of the divine nature*.

For this very reason make every effort to supplement your faith with virtue, and virtue with knowledge, and knowledge with self-control, and self-control with steadfastness, and steadfastness with godliness, and godliness with brotherly affection, and brotherly affection with love.

For if these things are yours and abound, they keep you from being ineffective or unfruitful in the knowledge of our Lord Jesus Christ. For whoever lacks these things is blind and shortsighted and has forgotten that he was cleansed from his old sins. Therefore, brethren, be the more zealous to confirm your call and election, for if you do this you will never fall. (II Peter 1:3-10.)

Thank you, Lord Jesus!

BIBLIOGRAPHY

(Note: Some authors write out of a previously established doctrine and others out of their own individual experience. We are never bound by another's experience, only by our own response to God's Word and His Spirit.)

Arnold, Eberhard, *The Experience of God and His Peace*, Plough Pub. House

Augsburger, Myron, *Quench Not the Spirit*, Choice Books

Barclay, Wm., *Flesh and Spirit*, Abingdon
  The Promise of the Spirit, Westminister Press

Bixler, Russell, *It Can Happen to Anybody*, Whitaker Books

Brown, Dale, W., *Flamed by the Spirit*, The Brethren Press

Bruce, F. F., Paul, *Apostle of the Heart Set Free*, Eerdmans

Damboriena, Prudencio, *Tongues as of Fire*, Corpus Books

Durasoff, Steve, *Bright Wind of the Spirit*, Prentice-Hall, Inc.

Graham, Billy, *The Holy Spirit*, Word

Hembree, Ron, *Fruits of the Spirit*, Baker Book House

Hession, Roy, *Be Filled Now*, Christian Literature Crusade

Kelsey, Jorstad, Mills, and Pulkingham, *A Charismatic Reader*, Religious Book Club

Kinghorn, Kenneth C., *Gifts of the Spirit*, Abingdon

Kinghorn, Kenneth C., *Fresh Wind of the Spirit*, Abingdon

Lehman, Chester K., *The Holy Spirit and the Holy Life*, Herald Press

Loomis, Earl A., M.D., *The Self in Pilgrimage*, Harper & Row

McConkey, Jas. H., *Three Fold Secret of the Holy Spirit*, Back to the Bible Broadcast

Marshall, Catherine, *The Helper*, Chosen Books

Nichol, John Thomas, *Pentecostalism*, Harper & Row

Oates, Wayne E., *The Holy Spirit in Five Worlds*, Associated Press

Pache, Rene, *The Person and Work of the Holy Spirit*, Moody Press

Quebedeaux, Richard, *The New Charismatics*, Doubleday

Seamands, David A., *Tongues Psychic and Authentic*

Sherrill, John L., *They Speak with Other Tongues*, Spire Books

Shoemaker, Samuel M., *With the Holy Spirit and With Fire*, Harper & Row

Stagg, Hinson & Oates, *Glossolalia*, Abingdon

Stewart, James S., *The Wind of the Spirit*, Abingdon

Stott, John R., *Baptist and Fullness*, Intervarsity Press

Underhill, Evelyn, *The Fruits of the Spirit*, Longman, Green & Co.

Van Dusen, Henry P., *Spirit, Son and Father*, Scribners

White, Ernest, M.D., *Christ and the Unconscious*, Harper & Row

114